# LEGACY SONG

## Your Supernatural Impact on Future Generations

Published by:

  Gateway Create Publishing
  www.gatewaycreate.com

Requests for publishing should be addressed to:
  Gateway Create Publishing
  500 South Nolen Suite #300
  Southlake TX, 76092

Scriptures taken from the New King James Version. Copyright © 1982 by Thomas Nelson, Inc. Used by permission. All rights reserved.
*ISBN:978-0-9898184-4-5*

While the incidents in this book represent actual events in the life of the author, in some instances their chronological order has been adjusted to fit within the timeline of the narrative. Pseudonyms have been used to protect the privacy of some individuals.

All the ends of the earth
Shall remember and turn to the LORD,
And all the families of the nations
Shall worship before You.
For the kingdom is the LORD's
And He rules over the nations.
Psalm 22:27–28

# Endorsements

I love Olen Griffing! I love him because he is a good father. I didn't say a perfect father, but a good one. A good father is known by the legacy of sons and daughters that come from his house, not the size of his house. By that record alone, Olen Griffing is a successful father. Healthy spiritual sons and daughters dot the world as a testimony to his life and legacy.

Like any good father, he knows how to weave the barbs of truth into stories that guide those who follow them on the path called life. Perhaps you feel a twinge of jealously that you didn't have this type of father in the faith. Don't despair. Now you can be parented by proxy through the stories he told his sons and daughters.

What I didn't know was that Olen could sing. I will have to listen a bit closer the next time I am in a worship service with him. In the meantime, the comforting syllables of his songs and stories have spoken peace to my heart in this hotel room in England.

Thank you, Olen. Thank you for continuing to sing. And for putting your song into print. I will rest well tonight. I may even laugh a bit.

Tommy Tenney
Founder and CEO of GodChasers.network

My regard for Pastor Olen Griffing runs deep. As you read *Legacy Song* and discover his wisdom, as you laugh along with his stories, and, after you've "caught" something of the true grit that makes great shepherds such as he exemplifies, I think you'll share my regard.

Pastor Jack Hayford, Founder
The King's University
Dallas – Los Angeles

If you want to read a book that will cause you to laugh, cry, and learn, this is the book for you.

*Legacy Song* is one of the most transparent books I have ever read. It is unpretentious, but it carries a burning message of our responsibility and privilege to nurture and develop future generations.

The book is written in a natural style that made it easy for me to picture this Texas-trooper-turned-pastor as he walked through his trials and experienced his victories.

Olen has a father's heart and is a true apostle. He pastored me through some difficult times in my own ministry. I believe his life is exemplary as one who loves, cares, and is faithful to the end. He has earned the right to counsel and instruct those of us who aspire to walk in such large footsteps.

I am delighted to recommend this book both for enjoyment and instruction. It is desperately needed by our generation.

Dr. Sue Curran
Founding Pastor Shekinah Church, Blountville Tennessee

Few leaders I've known in my over 30 years of ministry have produced the abundant fruit and lasting legacy that Pastor Olen Griffing has. The rich insights and stories from a leader who has "walked the walked" will have a profound impact on your life and leadership.

Jonathan Bernis, President and CEO
Jewish Voice Ministries, International

This is a book of captivating true-life tales, because the storyteller is remarkable. Pastor Olen Griffing's life adventures with God have the grip to command your attention and the power to change your life. I am humbled to call this pastor and friend my spiritual father. I was shaped as a young man listening to his sermons, serving under his leadership, and gleaning from his practical wisdom. It is impossible to separate Pastor Griffing from his stories, because they contain nuggets of truth, humor, and insight from his heart.

*Legacy Song* is the story of a man with an inspiring and lasting legacy who started from simple beginnings to impacting nations.

Pastor Olen has lived his life as a song poured out to God and others. Reading *Legacy Song*, you will be amused with laughter, sobered, and challenged. You will discover your own song and legacy.

Wayne Wilks, Jr., Ph.D.
President, Messianic Jewish Bible Institute

This book had to be written, should have been written, and needed to be written. It had to be because the story needed to be told by the man at the center of the story. It should have because the Body of Christ at large needed understanding of unknown components that made the story. It was needed because of people like me who knew sketches but not the whole story.

Thank you, Olen, for telling the story with love, humility, and grace in your own inimitable style. You make Jesus look ever better!

Remember with me a time many years ago when you thought I was there to encourage you and your deeply disappointed friends. Fact is, you were there to encourage me. It's our little secret that only heaven understands! Thank you!

Jack Taylor
Dimensions Ministries
Melbourne, Florida

# Table of Contents

# Acknowledgements

A very special thanks and deep appreciation to Mary Dunham Faulkner for the endless hours over the period of two years you spent with Syble and me, telling stories, praying together, laughing, crying, and working on this project in that Oklahoma cabin. What sweet memories! As you and I know, it would never have happened without you. Thanks from the bottom of my heart. Joe, you spent countless hours by yourself while Mary, Syble, and I worked through the details. Thanks.

Gary and Ruyana Fugitt, we are so grateful for the hours spent in your wonderful hideaway, the Peacock Inn, where we could pray, write, and contemplate as this book was being birthed. Thank you for your wonderful hospitality and friendship.

Our first home group at Shady Grove Church, Ron and Gayle Woods, Mimi and Gary Ribble, Ken and Barbara Smith, walked through most of these stories with us. Thank you for being there all these years, listening to crazy ideas, and praying us through many situations. You made life worth living many times.

Wayne and Bonnie Wilks, you are our heros. Your love, support, wisdom, and input have been invaluable. Thanks for encouraging us to do this book.

Shady Grove Elders, you were my rock. Thank you.

Last, but by far not least, our children, Jerri Benjamin and Mark Griffing, you walked these steps with us. We know it was not always easy, but thank you for believing in us. We love you both more than you can imagine . . . yes, you can . . . you have children.

I

# Foreword

When I finished reading *Legacy Song*, I called Pastor Olen and said, "I want you to know I blame you."

"What? What are you blaming me for?" he asked.

"For not letting me get any sleep last night. I started your book, and I couldn't put it down!"

Trust me, I know that's how you'll feel once you start reading this book.

Pastor Olen's legacy is one steeped in worship and guided by the Holy Spirit. For decades, Olen was the Senior Pastor of Shady Grove Church. I went on staff there when I was twenty-two years old, and it's where I grew up in the Spirit. It was home for me. I spent about sixteen years working with him, and he fathered me during tough times and good times, and even when God called my family to minister somewhere else.

When Pastor Olen talks about the importance of humility, I can testify to the validity of that principle in his life. The same goes for the principle of honoring those from past generations and finding freedom from generational iniquities. Not to mention the importance of prayer and worship. It's because of his influence in these areas that there's such an emphasis on freedom, prayer, and worship at Gateway Church. However, his influence goes even further than just me. It has been felt worldwide.

In fact, I have personally seen the influence Pastor Olen has had on thousands of people around the world as he has traveled to nearly every continent. The thing that makes his story even greater is when you look at his humble beginnings. I wonder what he would say if you had told him how important his legacy would become as he watched one of the first churches he pastored, Shady Grove Baptist Church, burn to the ground in the 70s. In the years that followed, he had to rebuild his dreams and rely on God's faithfulness every step of the way. I'm so glad I had the opportunity to walk alongside him for many of those years. More importantly, I'm so glad he instilled in me a legacy as a spiritual son.

Pastor Olen is a spiritual father to me, and like a good father, he tells great stories. As I read through *Legacy Song,* I laughed out loud at stories I've probably heard a hundred times, such as the humorous way God taught him how to truly worship or, when driving a green Gremlin, God taught him and his wife, Syble, about humility. I laughed like it was the first time I'd heard them. A good storyteller does that. They pull you into the story through humor while sharing personal experiences and deep truths about having a relationship with God. That's what *Legacy Song* is all about.

As you read this book, my hope is that you'll be inspired not only by Pastor Olen's experiences but by his challenge to embrace your own legacy. It's as simple as answering God's call and obeying Him. But just like Olen's story, what you'll leave behind will last for generations.

Robert Morris
Founding Senior Pastor, Gateway Church
Dallas/Fort Worth, Texas
Best selling Author of *The Blessed Life, From Dream to Destiny,
The God I Never Knew,* and *The Blessed Church*

# Introduction

The 1960s and 1970s marked a period of time when churches around the world experienced an outpouring of the Holy Spirit that came to be known as the Charismatic Movement. This movement was marked by dramatic, individual encounters with God, termed "the baptism with the Holy Spirit." But this was not new terminology. John the Baptist referred to Holy Spirit baptism in Matthew 3:11, saying, *"I indeed baptize you with water unto repentance, but He who is coming after me is mightier than I, whose sandals I am not worthy to carry. He will baptize you with the Holy Spirit and fire."*

Following the resurrection, Jesus also spoke to His followers about this experience when He commanded them not to depart from Jerusalem but to wait there for the Promise of the Father: *"But you shall receive power when the Holy Spirit has come upon you; and you shall be witnesses to Me in Jerusalem, and in all Judea and Samaria, and to the end of the earth"* (Acts 1:8).

The book of Acts records the initial outpouring of this promised experience: *When the Day of Pentecost had fully come, they were all with one accord in one place. And suddenly there came a sound from heaven, as of a rushing mighty wind, and it filled the whole house where they were sitting. Then there appeared to them divided tongues, as of fire, and one sat upon each of them. And they were all filled with the Holy Spirit and began to speak with other tongues, as the Spirit gave them utterance* (Acts 2:1–4).

With this initial outpouring came the supernatural legacy of faith that Jesus Himself bequeathed to that first generation of believers. It is a legacy that has since been passed to every succeeding generation of the Body of Christ. Although this supernatural legacy is available to all who believe, it is only accessible to those who seek it.

Olen Griffing was the son of a Baptist preacher who, after living life the way he wanted for a number of years, made his own commitment to God at the age of thirty-one. Inspired by the legacy of faith handed to him by his father, he enrolled in the second largest seminary in the country while working part-time to support his family. Upon graduation, Olen's dream of becoming a pastor came true.

But something was missing. Olen wanted something more; he wanted to know the supernatural God of the Bible. Olen Griffing went in search of something more, and ended up getting more than he expected. When he came face-to-face with the Spirit of the living God—the God of Abraham, Isaac, and Jacob—both religious tradition and the old Olen, along with all his flaws, mistakes, and sins, became a thing of the past. Olen had been set free.

But not everyone was happy about his newfound freedom. His church was burned to the ground, his denomination rejected him, and his family was virtually shunned by those who had once embraced and accepted them. Although everything in Olen's life was being shaken, his faith in a supernatural God remained firm.

Undeterred by events in the natural, Olen and a group of men and women from the church he pastored set out to rebuild. Not just a church, but rather a supernatural living legacy that would impact generations to come. Today, the children Olen has raised up (three generations of both natural and spiritual children) are scattered throughout the world, making a supernatural impact on their own generations.

The book you hold in your hands is Olen's story, his legacy song to you and to future generations. He believes the secret to impacting those around us is the way we respond to situations, both negative and positive ones. While your experience is not likely to be the same as Olen's, you have your own story—your own legacy song—that God desires to use to impact future generations . . . *supernaturally.*

# CHAPTER 1

# *Interrupted*

So there I was, bags packed and in the car, tickets in my right inside jacket, and my wife, Syble, ready to drive me to the Dallas/Fort Worth International Airport. I was scheduled for a 2:15 p.m. departure to Buenos Aires for a pastor's conference that had been on my calendar for months, and I was revved and ready. After all, I'd just finished a "three-sermon Sunday" at Shady Grove Church, so I was "practiced up." I didn't even think I needed my notes, but I'd packed them in my briefcase anyway. As they say in Texas, "I was ready for bear." Bring it on!

On the way to the airport, Syble said we should swing by Dr. Fong's to check out the ulcer pain I'd been having. No one, not even a doctor, would have called me sick. I almost argued her timing, but then decided against it. Sometimes it's good to have some strong anti-acids for these overseas trips, especially when staying and eating outside the city.

Two hours later, my American Airlines flight 997 to Argentina had an on-time departure—but I was not on it. Instead, I was staring at the sterile white ceiling in the cardiac care unit of Baylor Hospital, trying desperately to talk to the nurses. I told them nothing was wrong with me. I explained that hundreds of pastors and leaders were waiting for me in Argentina. "Whatever you're doing, could you please make it fast?" I pleaded.

No one listened as they snaked a tube down my throat, put another up my nose, hooked one into my arm, and poked an opening in my leg. They pried, pricked, and needled my body as they talked about cutting it open to get to my heart.

Whoa! My heart?

Okay, so I'd been a little breathy lately when I exercised. Had a little pain when I was using my weed eater the other day. But the doctor was talking about four clogged arteries, one at almost 100 percent. He said only drops of blood were getting to my heart, and he didn't understand why I was still alive.

This was all going way too fast, and I wanted everyone to slow down. I needed to think. I needed to pray about it—talk it over with my wife. I told the doctor I'd come back.

"Mr. Griffing," the heart surgeon said patiently, making sure I understood every word he was saying, "we can't guarantee your heart is going to last until tomorrow morning."

I'd been plucked up from my normal life with my normal plans and wheeled up to the edge of eternity. Life, as I had known it, had stopped.

I looked at my sweet wife and tried to press the pause button on all the thoughts and emotions flooding over me. Besides Jesus, she was my closest friend. But now I was going into this surgery, alone. I remember thinking either God would heal my heart or I was looking at her for the last time.

"I'll see you later, either here or there. I love you," I said.

She bent down, smiled, and kissed me tenderly on the part of my face that did not have a wire or hose taped to it. "I'll be right here when you get back," she said in her I-know-when-I'm-right voice. I knew she had no fear. Strangely enough, I didn't either. Whether I went to be with the Lord or stayed, I was at peace.

## Where and What?

It didn't take emergency heart surgery for me to know that life is fragile. I have taught and preached to congregations around the world with two major themes: eternity and worship. These themes are natural to me because, as humans, we were created to live forever and to worship. It's up to us to decide *where* we live and *what* we worship.

I've preached at enough funerals to know that each of us knows we won't live forever. "Life is short," we tell each other. But most of us don't think too much about what we're leaving behind when it's over.

It takes a strong focus to build an eternal legacy that will impact future generations. But the problem with doing so seems to be this: we're too busy surviving the world to think too much about eternity. There's the mortgage payment coming up, the higher price at the gas pump, and the cost of our kids' tuition. We have to make our marriages work, get along with our bosses, and keep our kids out of trouble. Who has time to think about legacy?

But if we're eternal beings (and we are), it makes sense to consider both eternity and legacy. The two go together.

My good friend Wayne Myers said it well: "We need to grasp of the brevity of life and the vastness of eternity." If we have these two facts lined up right in our life, we will make our decisions based on the eternal instead of "the need of now."

The legacy I want generations after me to have is a durable faith that will take my children—and theirs after them—through life and eternity. Of course, a fat, wealthy will would be nice. But in the end, our money and the things we own are the cheapest things we have—and the least expensive things we leave behind us. Who we are now and who we are becoming is ultimately the gift we will each leave behind.

The three greatest questions we will ever ask ourselves are:

Where am I going to live eternally?

Who am I becoming right now?

What do I want to leave behind for future generations?

## Authentic, Not Perfect

When Paul affirmed Timothy's faith, he said it lived in his grandmother first and then in his mother. And finally, Paul said, it was handed down and now lived in Timothy: *I call to remembrance the genuine faith that is in you, which dwelt first in your grandmother Lois and your mother Eunice, and I am persuaded is in you also* (2 Timothy 1:5).

Paul described Timothy's grandmother's faith as a sincere faith—not perfect. But it was authentic. It had to be the "never give up until the end" kind of faith for it to keep moving down the generations.

And sure enough, there's Lois's grandson showing up in the New Testament. Timothy's faith continues to move down through multiple generations. His life still serves you and me today. If you are a Christian, your faith has been strengthened by what he left behind. The New Testament has two books named for Timothy. Listen to Paul describing him: *For I have no one like-minded, who will sincerely care for your state. For all seek their own, not the things which are of Christ Jesus. But you know his proven character, that as a son with his father he served with me in the gospel* (Philippians 2:20–22).

That's eternal legacy.

Handing down your faith doesn't necessarily mean taking your kids to church (though if you're wise, you'll do it). A recent Barna Group poll found that less that 1 percent of the young-adult population in the United States has a biblical worldview. More shocking than this, less than one-half of 1 percent of Christians between the ages of eighteen and twenty-three have a biblical worldview.

We can tell people what we believe, and we can tell our children how they should live. That's easy. The world is full of people preaching, God bless them. But not many people can live off of sermons—inside the church or out. If they could, marriages and children would be perfect, and my pastor friends and I would all be national heroes. They're not; we're not.

What most of us are looking for is a life we can follow. How do we live a life of significance? How do we have hope when life keeps slamming us up against the wall? How do we stay passionate about our dream when it has turned into a nightmare? How do we hold on to faith when you see no evidence of it working?

Every time we overcome the evil around us, we carve out steppingstones for generations after us. Every time we stand up (again), in spite of the mess around us, we are creating a spiritual roadmap for others to follow. Children and adults in generations to come will use our roadmap to make it home safely.

As for me, before they laid my heart out on a surgery table, I could have given you a long list of what I wanted out of life. That was fifteen years ago. Since then, I've narrowed the list down to two things: (1) I want to love God, and (2) I want to love His people.

It's funny how life and values can be condensed into time capsules— moments and pictures that stay with us forever. In my case, one such moment was when I came out of heart surgery and realized I was alive.

The first person I saw was my beautiful daughter, Jerri. She was hovering and fretting like I wasn't there. I was trying to get her attention, but she was too busy talking to the nurse.

"He wants something," she said. "What does he want?"

The nurse saw my hand flopping in the air; it was the only thing I could move. "He wants you to hold his hand."

And the nurse was right. I needed to feel the touch of someone I loved and who loved me back. My daughter caressed my hand and her daughter, Courtney, rubbed my hair like I was a pet poodle. "You're going to be all right, Dandy," she cooed over me.

I had taught my daughter to intercede and pray. She had taught her daughter the same thing. And there they were in the hospital room, pouring their faith and love right back at me, just when I needed it the most.

The seeds Syble and I have planted keep growing—in our children and in the lives of those we've taught and mentored throughout years of ministry. Most of them are like strong oak trees now, with branches reaching out to the nations. And I get to live and enjoy it: legacy multiplying.

# CHAPTER 2

## Legacy's Song

When I was in high school, I was a full-fledged member of SPEBSQSA. Not impressed? Not many people are. The Society for the Preservation and Encouragement of Barber Shop Quartet Singing in America has not taken over the world.

But I loved being a part of it. In fact, anything to do with music has always been my thing. In high school, I joined the mixed ensemble, the male quartet, the male choir, the concert choir, the a cappella choir, and the touring choir—anything that had notes and harmony. All that training paid off when I was asked to sing a solo for President Lyndon Johnson's private family funeral in Johnson City, Texas.

We always mark the happy and sad and everything-in-between moments of our life with music. From the cradle to the grave, music connects our personal history. We sing over brand-new babies when they first come into the world. (Syble used to sing "Rock-a-bye-Baby," which didn't make sense to me. Our babies would snuggle up to her and fall asleep while she was singing words like "when the bough breaks, the cradle will fall, and down will come baby, cradle and all.")

When children get older, we take them to recitals and band practices and haul them to music lessons. When they get married, we dance to love songs and sing in the New Year with "Auld Lang Syne." We belt out the "Star Spangled Banner" at our ball games (and if you're like me, you get a lump in your throat every time). "We Shall Overcome" is the history-changing song Martin Luther King used to change a nation.

Music started in heaven, way before we came on the scene. We get our love for music from a musical God. Job speaks of morning stars singing together (see Job 38:7). Jesus sang with His disciples (see Mark 14: 26), and the Holy Spirit worships God through us with song (see Ephesians 5:18 and Hebrews 2:12).

Music is God's signature, He's stamped it everywhere. Even on us, personally. Every life moves with a melody and rhythm that other people can hear and see. Sometimes we can hear the sound of each other, in spite of the words we say.

Don't believe me? Listen to your iPhone. There's a Looney Tunes melody for the crazy boss, a love song for our spouse (if we're smart), and a heavy dirge tone to alert us to the friend who loves to give advice. "Here it comes," we say as we brace ourselves.

If you're someone who can't let go of the past, what music people hear when they're around you is the country version of "Another Somebody Done Somebody Wrong Song." And if you're an angry person, your hard-as-rock notes bang up the people around you.

Although we may not be aware of the fact, music molds our identity and even our theology. Just as God has a song, Satan also has his. If we listen to his lyrics and the twisted, angry melody, we can tell the difference.

Our enemy Satan, used to be the choir director in heaven. When he wants to turn us away from God, he uses music. When he wants to shape a culture with doubt, he first sets his message to the tune of music and then he adds the lyrics. Once we look back on our short life span from an eternal perspective, we will see that the enemy always had a plan to change us into a people of bondage.

My wife and I recently watched the Academy Award-winning *Les Miserables*, and I was so moved that I cried more than she did. Victor Hugo's story, first written in 1862, still sings clearly about law and grace, truth and justice, good and evil. "Do You Hear the People Sing?" could be the prophetic anthem of any nation whose people stand up for freedom.

If we want to be free, we have to first decide we won't be slaves. If we want our children and generations after us to know our freedom, we can't be passive about changes that reflect a culture that does not know its Creator.

Worship is the song that began in heaven, at the throne of God. We sing it on earth even though it has a different rhythm from the one around us. We march triumphantly and live resolutely because we hear a different drumbeat. The life that emerges out of worship conquers darkness and injustice on earth, in all of its forms.

On the day Moses died, God told him to write a song. So there Moses was, trying to say his good-byes, planning his funeral, and writing the notes and lyrics to his own song. It was a busy time, this death. Forty years earlier, he had sung a victory song after he and the children of Israel crossed the Red Sea. But this song was to be his last song—his legacy song—written by Moses and God Himself.

One thing was clear from the start: This was not going to be some kumbaya kind of music where God and Moses held hands and swayed together. No, this was God penning strong lyrics of warning and strong lyrics of love, all at the same time. This song included the law and the prophetic, human nature and sin—subjects that don't tend to make it to the top of the music charts. Nobody was going to be doing a hip-hop dance to these lyrics. Through this song, God told His people, "Listen, I know you forget easily. You're human. And when you drift, you don't tend to drift toward Me. You tend to drift away from Me, and truth,

9

and goodness." God knew ahead of time that in future generations the great temptation for all of us would be shaped and molded by the culture around us, not by the Word of God.

He's God. He remembers that we are dust. When life is tough, people tend to blame God. When it's not, they sometimes forget God. When life is bitter, some curse God. God is not shocked. Rather, He hums the words to the song He and Moses wrote for us thousands of years before. He reminds us through a song who He will always be: *He is the Rock, His work is perfect; For all His ways are justice, A God of truth and without injustice; Righteous and upright is He* (Deuteronomy 32:4).

At the cross, Jesus picked up Moses' legacy song and mixed it with grace and forgiveness. Jesus didn't change the song; He just made the notes sweeter, easier to sing: *For the law was given through Moses, but grace and truth came through Jesus Christ* (John 1:17).

Listen to Moses and Jesus singing a duet near the end of Revelation:

> They sing the song of Moses, the servant of God, and the song of the Lamb, saying:
> *"Great and marvelous are Your works,*
> *Lord God Almighty!*
> *Just and true are Your ways,*
> *O King of the saints!*
> *Who shall not fear You, O Lord, and glorify Your name?*
> *For You alone are holy.*
> *For all nations shall come and worship before You,*
> *For Your judgments have been manifested"* (Revelation 15:3–4).

If you're a believer, you've got this song inside you. God is your rock (when the world is wobbly). He is just (when you've been betrayed).

He is faithful (when friends forsake you). There is no iniquity in Him. Period. When we know this, we pass it down.

Our culture is cracked open and confused. It cries out for answers: Who is God? How many gods are there? Is God a he or a she? Can't I just worship the universe and cover all my bases? These are honest questions of still-searching hearts.

Our world needs the clear, precise sound of a people who know their Redeemer and sing His song to another generation:

> *That the generation to come might know them,*
> *The children who would be born,*
> *That they may arise and declare them to their children,*
> *That they may set their hope in God,*
> *And not forget the works of God,*
> *But keep His commandments* (Psalm 78:6).

We are not responsible for making everything turn out right for everybody. Our identity is not wrapped up in how many people hear or follow us. We can't control life and people's decisions and choices.

But we can keep our sound pure. We can get back to the right key when we get off track. We can keep putting our legacy song in our children's mouths. We can keep singing over the darkness instead of stepping into it.

As believers, we are smart when we ask questions of ourselves:

What if we lived our life finding out more about who God is?

What if we could sing the same song God and Moses wrote?

What if we learned how to use the instrument of our life to create joy in our generation?

What if we made the next big or small decision in the light of eternity?

I'm just asking. *What if?*

# CHAPTER 3

# *Hand-me-downs*

When she was young, my mother had jet-black hair with a natural white streak running through it—like she had just had it done at a beauty salon. She was a striking woman with a good figure; men almost always looked twice—and Mom didn't discourage it.

She was raised in a home without self-esteem, healthy love, or nurturing, and the only version of family she knew was a fantasy image of what families should be. When she married at the age of fifteen and became a mother at sixteen. Her plastic-pretend replica of a family was all she had to hand down to my sister and me. Still, I loved her. I thought if I could please her, she would love and nurture me, and everything would be all right. But that dream would never be. Instead, she raised me and my sister like we were in the military. She was the sergeant and my sister and I, the scared soldiers. We could get busted at any moment.

Shirts were to be hung exactly two fingers apart, underwear stacked in perfect squares. Socks had to be store-bought-spaced according to color, and ready for inspection at any time. "Olen, come back in here and straighten up your sock drawer," she would yell through the house. There could be no dust—ever—and when she got home from work, she checked the kitchen cupboard to see if I had taken out a cup. If so, had I put it back in the right space?

On Saturdays I did laundry, hung the clothes to dry on lines in our backyard, and then took them down later to fold and, sometimes, iron. I balked at my lack of freedom, and when I asked to play with my friends, Mom always had a reason why I couldn't. It always had to do with what "others" would think: What would *they* think of the dust on the furniture and the un-mopped floors? What if *they* opened my sock drawer? What if I were in a wreck and didn't have clean underwear on—what would *they* think?

None of this reasoning made sense to me. What about just relaxing and sitting in the living room like other families did? What about wearing clean underwear just because I wanted to?

We lived in a plastic fortress that looked so good from the outside, no one knew we needed some help.

Dad was tenderhearted; he loved God and loved his family. But he couldn't change his wife and never figured out how to make things right in his home. I loved him like crazy and was always proud of him anyway. Divorce was not an option for him; his strong commitment to his family and to God was the gift that made up for everything else.

We all lived with secrets that were too big to unravel or understand, so we just lived. "Do the best you can with what you've got" was Dad's unspoken message. So I did. And it worked—as long as I remembered I would be able to leave home one day.

Until then, I lived with Mom's secrets and a regimen that, years later, would prepare me for the Army Reserve.

It would be years before I was freed of the resentment that formed and cemented inside me from those years with Mom. Love looked twisted and malformed and had no safe spots for rest. But if I wanted another version of home, I would have to make my own. The one I had wasn't changing.

## Cut the Chain

The life that is handed down to each of us is just that: handed down. None of us get a sign-up sheet to check where and when we want to be born. We don't choose our lineage or the environment we're raised in. It is what it is—love it or hate it—you can't change your parent's legacy.

The Bible speaks of both blessings and sins going down through generations. I don't know of any parents who purposefully drop curses on babies and set out to harm their young. And I haven't met many people who brought children into the world and then raised them perfectly. (If you're one of those people who have no scars or regrets from childhood, go in peace. You are blessed.) The rest of us have to make sure our parents' sins don't stick to our spirits and mark us for life.

Time seldom heals the scars from our childhood. We can hide them and push them down and declare them gone. But eventually, we have to decide we want to be healed and take responsibility to clean up the mess left to us. Unfortunately for us, blaming our mom and dad has never been the key to wholeness.

## Long Life and Hidden Blessings

In one of my Wednesday night Bible studies, a businessman, still in his suit and tie from work, slipped into class and sat stoically through the teaching. He was tall and distinguished, and seemed like a man of authority. Afterwards, when he asked me to pray for him, I was surprised that he could hardly speak. Instead, he started weeping with deep emotion as he declared, "I hate my father!" Those four words were an introduction, a statement, and prayer request all at the same time. It was as if he couldn't carry the weight of his heart anymore, and he'd come to class to dump it.

15

I didn't know him, but I recognized the pain immediately. I felt great compassion for a heart that didn't want to hate. After we prayed, I shared my story with him, along with three of the keys that had unlocked my own healing.

## Key #1: Release Your Parents

It doesn't matter what your parents did or didn't do to you or for you. If you want to hand something down other than what they left you, you have to make a choice to forgive. Let it go.

Sometimes forgiveness sounds like a cliché. We preach about it in a message, hear about it in sermons, and offer it as advice to our friends. Most of us know forgiveness is the path to freedom. We know we should forgive. We say we do. And yet our hearts don't seem to get the message.

In order to understand forgiveness in its full power, we first have to experience it. God's pattern of forgiveness was made manifest to mankind through Jesus Christ. Because He wiped the slate clean for each of us, we now have the power to erase the stain of someone else's sin against us.

Sometimes, our parents' sins are the hardest to forgive. We hold our fathers and mothers accountable for our DNA and for who we are and how they shaped us. Some people blame their parents for their scars, for their bad relationships, and even for their present actions. The message is, "If you don't like me, blame my parents; they made me this way." After all, who asked to be born?

But eventually we have to release our parents from our expectations of how we wanted to be raised, and quit judging them for what they did or didn't do. The facts seem cold and brutal, and we hate to face them, but we are responsible for our choices, for how we love and whom we forgive.

## Key #2: Honor Is a Verb

God knew this parent-child relationship would be an issue for all of us, for all time. That's why He addressed it right at the beginning. In fact, this subject made it to number four of His Ten Commandments in Exodus 20:12: *"Honor your father and your mother."* And just to make sure we wouldn't forget, He brought it up again in the New Testament: *"Honor your father and mother," which is the first commandment with promise: "that it may be well with you and you may live long on the earth"* (Ephesians 6:1–3).

Obviously, like all good parents, God has a few family rules, and this one is straightforward and to the point: respect and honor your parents. You've probably already noticed the command and blessing don't come with pre-existing conditions. You've never heard God say, "To get respect, you have to earn it." That's one of those sayings that has been around so long, it sounds like Scripture. But it's not. God just says, "Honor them."

The fourth commandment is not God's attempt to make life more painful for us. He's telling us He has picked up the tab for our parents' lack. He's the Father of the fatherless, the abused, and the rejected, who is saying, "I'll give you the kind of life you want and the years to enjoy it. But you have to honor the people who gave you life." He is the original parent who is the great model of love and sacrifice for His own children. We know Him because His Son, Jesus, introduced us to God as His parent who loves so much He can't help Himself. He gives us everything we need and deeply desire, just not when and how we think it should be. Fair enough, I say.

When you think about it, that's good parenting.

## Key #3: Give Thanks

One of the most profound verses in the Bible is in 1 Thessalonians 5:18: *In everything give thanks; for this is the will of God in Christ Jesus for you.* This one verse in the New Testament has become a way of living for me. When I need to sort out my priorities, I first give thanks. When I need to know the will of God, I give thanks. When I want joy, I give thanks. And when I want to honor anyone, I count the ways I'm thankful for that person.

Just as we recount our parent's offenses (sometimes for years), we can decide to give thanks for anything and everything they did right. In fact, trust me, even when you think there is nothing to thank God for about one or both of your parents, when the Holy Spirit binds up your spirit, He will also direct your heart to look for the good He deposited in them.

I've made a list of things about Mom that I thank God for. With her seventh grade education and a history of abuse, she did the best she could. She survived. She never left me or my sister or my father, although she couldn't have been a happy woman. She never knew how to get healed, but she never gave up. As much as I hated our relationship and the abuse, the discipline and order she put in me has served me well in my life and ministry. She never let us children look dirty or tattered, and she made sure we got to school every day.

Mom is in a nursing home in Seattle now. Her body is worn out and her soul is still laden with her secrets. I visit her and talk about the things that make her happy. I pray with her every time I visit. I talk to her about eternity and being prepared to live there. I don't bring up the past; it is not our friend.

But long before she moved to a nursing home, my family welcomed Mom into our home, and we visited hers. We learned how to serve her and bypass the personality that, over the years, had hardened in its twisted form. Now that she is dying, we have no regrets. Although a warm relationship was not possible, love still trumped the day.

According to Scripture, the best thing you can do for yourself and your future is to forgive and honor your parents. The best thing you can do for your great-great-grandchildren is to spread forgiveness and thanksgiving all over your past. Your choice to forgive, honor, and give thanks will grow into your present and enlarge your future.

None of us parent perfectly, and whether we like it or not, our children will also have to forgive us for ways we never knew we hurt them. It just happens this way. We do the best we can, but most of us leave some unmet needs and unfulfilled expectations in our children.

When you sow forgiveness and love and compassion into your parents, God will give you the same thing in return. There will be a day when your children will forgive you and recount your ways with thankfulness and understanding. If it's not today, then wait for it. And while you're waiting for them to discover what you've planted in them, spread a thankful heart over them. Count the ways you love them and tell them often how much you care.

You and I can't change the past. But we don't have to live under its curse or hand it down to another generation.

# CHAPTER 4

# *Legacy in Progress*

I met the woman of my dreams when I was nineteen, when both of us were studying at Hardin Simmons University. Syble says she knew from the first time she saw me, she wanted to marry me. I felt the same way about her.

Poor Syb. She had no way of knowing she had just set her sights on one mixed-up guy whose looks and charm may have been the only two things going for him. When I discovered I could make good grades without studying, I was free to focus on my main goal: fun—and lots of it. Give me some excitement!

Four months after Syble and I met, we got married. I liked marriage at first—why wouldn't I? I was out of my mother's house and away from my dad's convictions. I felt free. The problem was, I kept celebrating. I frequently left my young wife at home and went out on the town with the guys, pretending I was not a married man.

After a while, marriage began to feel like another cage, and I wanted to leave the door open. So I did. Later, when we had our children, I still went out on the town with the guys. I didn't know the first thing about being a daddy and didn't try to learn. Syble stayed home with the children, and that was okay by me. I figured that was "her place." After all, she was my helpmate. To me, that meant she was to take care of the house and the kids and have dinner ready when I came home. That's what a woman does for her man.

I knew I was breaking my wife's heart. But I kept telling myself that at least I had never turned into a drunk; I had never gotten a girl pregnant, never done anything really bad like some of my friends.

I just needed more freedom than most people. What was so wrong with that?

Of course, Syble found plenty wrong with it. And I didn't like the guilt or the arguments we had when I walked back into the house. I finally realized I needed to leave her. I needed to be really free.

I hated the idea of telling her, but it had to be done. I figured I only had to have one hard conversation and it would be over. Even before I said anything, the words felt heavy in my mouth—like I was chewing on gravel. I dropped them out, fast and clumsy.

"Syble, I'm sorry, but I don't love you anymore."

We both stood there for a minute staring at each other. I waited for the tears. I knew they would come and I deserved them. I expected she would remind me of her love for me, of how God felt about my decision, how she felt about my decision. I expected her to talk about our wedding day, our vows and covenant. She would say, "Shame on you," and I would say, "Yes, shame on me."

I was ready. Or so I thought.

Instead of shedding tears, Syble started laughing. It started out as a chuckle and then turned into genuine belly laughter. Like I had just told her the funniest joke she ever heard.

"Oh, Olen," was all she managed to get out of her mouth. She was doubled over, hitting her thigh while waves of obvious hilarity convulsed her.

We now had a situation. For one thing, what I said wasn't funny. And, two, Syble thought it was. I was confused at first, and then agitated. Who responds to this kind of news like this? Was she making fun of me? I pointed out that nobody was laughing but her.

"I'm serious, Syble."

"Oh, Olen," she gasps between great guffaws of merriment. "You do too love me. Don't be silly. I know you do."

What kind of woman doesn't even know when she's not loved? There was nothing to say. Nothing I could think of to do. I left the house in a huff but later came back for dinner. Both of us eventually settled back into our old ways. I kept going out, and Syble kept being there when I got home.

## Confident Love

It turned out that Syble knew more about real love than I did. She had grown up in a home filled with unconditional love from both of her parents, so her confidence was a lifeline we both used at the same time—like an oxygen hose she was sharing with me.

I didn't know how to be a husband and father, and it showed. For me, love was mixed up with abuse and confusion and trauma. Even though I had "walked down the aisle" like every other Baptist did to receive Christ, I didn't really know Him. And at the time, I didn't know me either. That combined ignorance almost cost me everything.

But Syb was raised by a dad who had poured so much respect and love into her, that even then she stood strong and sure of who she was. This calm confidence is one of the most beautiful things a woman ever wears. And it was this confidence, along with some much-needed parenting that came from Syble's parents, that set me on a path to my own personal healing and the strengthening of our marriage.

If it had been left up to me, I would have handed down a legacy of brokenness and pain that would have pockmarked the future for my children, my grandchildren, and my great-grandchildren. Today, they are my most loved relationships on earth. I shudder to think of the impact my selfishness and sin could have had on all of them. Not that they are getting a perfect specimen of sainthood, even now, after all these years. But, thank God, I'm not what I used to be.

"The worst of sinners" is how the apostle Paul described himself at one point in his life. Another time he called himself "the least of the apostles." And somehow, I think he probably wasn't just trying to be humble.

Paul was an educated man who had grown up in the synagogue under one of the most prestigious rabbis of that time: Gamaliel. Paul was fluent in Hebrew, Greek, and Aramaic, but he was also full of hate, pride, and selfish ambition. He was a terrorist to the Church, hunting down and persecuting Christians without cause. In fact, when Christ confronted him, He told Paul he wasn't only persecuting His people; he was persecuting Jesus Christ Himself. That was a hard fact to live with. That could have been the legacy Paul left the world, but he changed it.

Chances are, the legacy you're leaving behind could use some tweaking. Or maybe your legacy needs some out-and-out change. The apostle Paul shows us three elementary keys we can use to turn our legacy around: face it, forget it, and fast forward.

## Key #1: Face It

Whatever your personal history may be, it's done. Putting your personal spin on your personal history won't change the fact that you've done some things wrong. Nobody—not Jesus, not even Paul himself—tried to honey-glaze the facts of Paul's life. He'd done what he'd done. Paul never tried to soft-pedal the fact that his zeal for what he believed had cost people their lives and devastated communities.

Sometimes, the greater our sin, the greater our story as we spin it later. But history has a way of untangling the facts and being objective about the truth even if we can't. Eventually, we have to face who we are and who we have been, with all our flaws and sins. Paul shows us how to be open and transparent. He was what he was: the chief of sinners. He was a violent man, a terrorist, before Christ transformed him.

## Key #2: Forget It

Facing our sins and the ugliness of our past is usually devastating. Like Paul, facing what we've done and who we've been oftentimes drops us to our knees, which is a good place to be. Redemption is offered at the cross and covers us completely—not only our present and future, but also our past.

If sin is behind you, keep it behind you. Paul says we are to forget it: *Brethren, I do not count myself to have apprehended; but one thing I do, forgetting those things which are behind and reaching forward to those things which are ahead, I press toward the goal for the prize of the upward call of God in Christ Jesus* (Philippians 3:13–14). The past has a hitching post of failure where some people firmly tie their reins. But no one successfully lives out his or her destiny by looking back. We may learn lessons from past failures, but we can't let ourselves remain tied to them.

When Satan tries to beat you down with guilt and bad memories, you have to remind both him and yourself: that was before the cross; this is now.

According to Paul, there wasn't just one thing he needed to forget. There were multiple things. Until the day we die, we all will wish we had done some things differently. Why did I say that? we may ask ourselves in disbelief after an argument. Why didn't I take more time? How did I fall into that sin again?

There is only one thing to do: face the truth and obey what the Holy Scripture and the Holy Spirit tell you to do. Make new history. We move toward maturity by hearing and obeying God—now.

25

Time doesn't heal our inward man or our past. We learn to keep taking our new failures to God and letting Him heal and cleanse. Then we move on.

## Key #3: Fast Forward

We can't build a great legacy overnight. It takes a lifetime to shape the legacy we will leave behind us. This is great news when we think about it. If we don't like what we're handing down to our children and across the span of future generations, we have time to change it.

The Bible is a book filled with legacies and true-to-life stories that show us how to shape our own lives and legacies. In Hebrews 11, we're introduced to men and women who changed the legacies they were handing down after them. Some of these saints were at the beginning of their lives, others were in the middle, and some were at the end. But the eternal impact of their lives was all the same. Although their lives spanned thousands of years and multiple generations, because of their individual faith, they changed history. That's encouraging to me and, hopefully, it is to you too.

I've learned from all of their lives. I don't fret over what should have been or even what could be. Instead I'm following Paul in this objective: *that I may know Him and the power of His resurrection, and the fellowship of His sufferings, being conformed to His death* (Philippians 3:10).

If we put all of our energy into knowing more of Christ Jesus, there won't be a whole lot of time for regrets, worry, and condemnation. It would be a worthless use of our time to relive, justify, or try to explain what was or could have been.

Just as we have to be careful not to berate ourselves with the "what ifs" and "should haves" regarding our past, we also have to be careful not to create a fantasy future built on "whens" and "ifs." It would be pointless to do so. We would be defrauding our own heart and others around us by living in a pretend future.

I'm thankful I've learned not to focus on the past or write checks on my future. I've learned how to live out my days in a relaxed relationship with God. I'm enjoying my "now" with Him. Every morning, I submit to His will for my life. I sit in His presence. I ask questions. I pour out my heart. And then I follow His guidance. I've decided I don't want to live with a made-up version of God or me. I want to pass down the real thing.

# CHAPTER 5

∽

# *Could I Have This Dance?*

Syble is the one of the few people I know who is completely happy with her childhood. When she relates this to others, people automatically think she's living in denial and needs a little reality therapy.

But even if she tries, she can't conjure up any memories of fighting or divorce or rejection. There simply aren't any. There are no family addiction stories, no abuse, and no emotional or physical neglect.

Her mom and dad had only one child, so she was doted on, for sure. They lived in Kermit, Texas, a spot on the road before the oil boom. I tell her she grew up good because there was no place for her to sin. In Kermit, everything stayed in order: God (who lived at First Baptist), family (who stayed together no matter what), and friends (who would never leave you because they had no place to go).

Besides Sunday morning church services, there were sing-a-long parties and potluck dinners with buttered biscuits and the daily news all served up together. In Kermit, you kept up with two things, your taxes and your neighbor's business: who did what, with whom, and where. That's how people knew you cared.

It may have been a small world, but it was secure. There was plenty of everything to go around: God, love, laughter, and friends. Syble had no way of knowing her future would take some sharp, hold-your-breath kind of turns.

What should have given her a clue was when, at age twelve, she went to the altar and dedicated her life to be a pastor's wife. What twelve-year-old girl tells God she wants to help take care of His people? But Syble knew what she knew. Her pastor confirmed her call and prayed over her. After the service, the members of Kermit's First Baptist Church shook her hand at the altar and blessed her.

Now, we both look at that strange experience and realize it was a prophetic glimpse into her destiny. Call me crazy, but I know God knew I needed Syble, and Syble needed me. Even as children, He was preparing us to be together.

Her parents are my heroes, and until they died, Syble and I loved hanging out with them. We both just enjoyed being around them because they loved Jesus, ball games, buttered biscuits, and having lots of fun.

But my wife's background of nurturing and love and fun never prepared her for what she had signed up for. Although being a pastor was not on my radar screen when Syble and I met, what she saw in me was a preacher's kid who had attended church and led worship. She's the one who thought I was going to be a preacher. When we entered the ministry together years later, I realized it was Syble's loving upbringing that prevented her from relating to the broken and addicted. Why on earth would people act mean when they didn't have to? Why did they cry so much? Why call yourself a Christian and then backbite? Why keep going down to the altar if God answered you the first time? To Syble, love meant loyalty. Faith meant faithfulness. She had little patience with hypocrisy.

## God Knows What We Need

I'm convinced God knows how to mix our DNA with the roots and family of the spouse He chooses for us. I needed the wholeness of Syble's parents to mentor me, and she needed my family and our mixed bag of dysfunction to grow her up in the ways of God and people. It sounds outrageous (even to my ears), but I believe my part of the family—including my abusive mother and my mother's soul-sick father before her—was crucial in my wife's life and call. Even my alcohol-addicted uncle taught us how to have empathy and understanding for the broken and bruised. I learned firsthand how God uses our families to teach and shape us.

Compassion and grace often come from the deep place of pain and sin that God has healed in our lives, and I've had plenty of both. Mercy has been just what I needed to minister to God's broken people. But Syb keeps my mercy gift in check with a kind of flat-footed reality that saves and protects us both.

For instance, Syble still loves to laugh and have fun, so most people don't know about her razor-sharp discernment. But she can tell if someone is the real deal or a good-sounding replica. She knows, as we say in Texas, if someone is "all hat without cattle."

In my earlier years of ministry, I wanted to live like the homeless—to really feel their pain and know what it was like to sleep on the streets. Syble, God love her, needed no such experiment. "Olen, don't be ridiculous. Are you going to do drugs so you can know how an addicts feel?" Of course, she had a point.

She doesn't bat an eye when I tell her I want to give all our money away to a missionary or hesitate when I tell her we're getting on the plane to go be one. We've done both, and she is always willing, always ready. She's a unique breed of a pastor's wife, rugged enough to ride the open plains of ministry with me and pretty enough to do a two-step when we need to have fun.

31

Over the years I've seen what look like mismatched couples—spouses that just don't seem to go together. You've met them too. One is outgoing and stylish, the other withdrawn and frumpy. Sometimes, one is sensitive and caring, the other obtuse, like they don't have a clue. And some men and women who are deeply spiritual are married to a mate who never wants to go to church or talk about God.

It doesn't always look like it, but God has a way of matching us with the spouse we need for the long haul of eternity. He knows us—really knows us—and not like we know each other. He is the beginning and the end in all things. He knows the family lineage intimately, who started what with whom and why. He sees the great-great-great-grandparents all across the generations to the great-great-great-grandchildren after them—all as one family unit. "I am the God of Abraham, Isaac and Jacob," He says. None of us were born at a stop-and-go light. We come from lineage.

## The Deal Breaker

Divorce breaks this line and drops family blessings. When we sever our "God-tie" with each other and drop our covenant vows, strengths and traditions are also left by the wayside.

Don't misunderstand me. I don't judge my divorced friends. Thank God for grace and forgiveness. Thank God for causing all things to work together for good, even when we fail. And thank God that He knows how to make all things new. I have seen God redeem divorce over and over. The beauty and love that come out of our pain prove God can take the hard things in life and turn them for our good. When you remarry after getting out of a bad marriage, you have to start working again on what may be different issues. But sometimes they turn out to be the same ones that took you down the first time. Only this time, everyone (parents, children, and grandchildren alike) starts over with different bloodlines. New

32

rules, new people, and newly broken pieces are handed down. Children and traditions and family albums change. But love and forgiveness are still needed.

Honoring your marriage covenant and staying inside the boundaries of its sacred vows are eternal decisions that will reap eternal results. Even if your marital past is pockmarked and stained, there is still time to be healed and to create the relationship your heart longs for. You can still hand down a lineage of faithfulness.

The marriage covenant we make in the eyes of God and man mirrors the relationship of the Holy Trinity. Can you imagine one Person of the Trinity walking away from the other two? Can you imagine the mess you and I would be in if that happened? But they can't walk away. They won't. They are the original and forever *one* God. The unity in the Holy Trinity is the pattern for our marriages, families, and nations, but we can only mirror it on earth by His Spirit. True unity is a heart condition that laws have never been able to legislate.

Marriage makes its best sense when we remember we are eternal beings. We will always need a supernatural love to enable us to hold on to our covenant to the end. When we view marriage as nothing more than a means of creating our own personal happiness rather than a covenant relationship established to glorify God, we need to do some rethinking. The destiny and fulfillment of God's call in our lives is connected to the other person in our marriage. Our spouse has what we need to sharpen and teach us. God is more than able to take two people in a difficult relationship and, if they are willing, mold and shape them in such a way that they will fulfill not only their commitment to each other but His plan and purpose for their lives as well.

Most of us have to develop the fruit of the Holy Spirit in the midst of the daily grind of life—the ups and downs of our marriage relationship. Who wouldn't want to receive patience kindness, longsuffering, and humility in a ten-minute altar call? But these are not gifts; they are fruit. They are qualities that have to be seeded and nurtured and grown in us. It's not an overnight process.

Pretty soon, if you love long enough, you get it. You understand that the process of developing the fruit of the Spirit is not about your spouse and what that person does or doesn't fulfill in you. It's about you—what God is shaping in you, who He is creating you to be, and where He's preparing to take you. When you submit to this process— and keep yielding to it—your life takes on a fragrant aroma that lingers long after you've left the living room of your life.

I haven't seen too many perfect marriages. Make that none. But there's something beautiful about two people who hold on to each other no matter what. They take the good, the bad, and the ugly in each other and mix it with everything the Holy Spirit provides. The fleshed-out example of this kind of union says everything about the legacy we want to leave to our children. Never give up.

## Me and My Gal

Syb and I have been married since January 1958. We've raised two children whom we both love like crazy. We have six grandchildren and eleven greats who've given us more joy than we dreamed possible. We haven't asked, but we are pretty sure both our kids had their children just to make us happy. (I could be wrong on that, but either way, we get to enjoy them.) We've ministered together in the same church for thirty-eight years and traveled around the globe from Jerusalem to Africa together. We still take romantic cruises and have fun, laugh-till-you-hurt dates.

And yes, we still have a good, strong argument from time to time. We need them; they keep our hearts honest and our communication real. There are times when Syb gets on my last nerve, and she says I sometimes drive her crazy too (but I can't see how). Either way, do you think either one of us would have missed this trip we're on?

When I talk to couples who are tempted to give up on their vows, I don't preach. I know they are hurting. Instead, I ask them a few questions: What if by being faithful during the hard times you could leave something sturdy and strong to pass on down after you? What if the trial you are going through today in your marriage is preparing you for something great in your future?

When we first fell in love, Syble and I danced to a golden oldie, entitled "Could I Have This Dance?" If you want to hand down a legacy of healing to your children and future generations, then make the choice to love—no matter what. And if you're going to pick a love song at the beginning of your relationship, don't do a weak, schmaltzy one. Choose one you can dance to for the rest of your life.

# CHAPTER 6

∞

# *Stick 'Em Up*

After Syble and I got married, I applied for a job as a Texas state trooper. I completed five months of strict training, and the day I got my badge, I felt like I was wearing all the power of the state of Texas. Every now and then I touched the handle of my gun, holstered on my right hip, just to make sure it was still there. Yep. Sure enough, I had turned myself into a person of the law.

A funny thing happened every time I put on that uniform. When I walked down the street, people treated me differently. The nice ones would smile and say hello, and the mean ones looked down at their shoes. Kids looked up at me with awe, like I was a form of Batman with superpowers. Everybody in town treated me with respect. I knew I was going to like this job.

I was young and green, but I had enough sense not to abuse this power. I was honored to serve the United States in general, and the state of Texas in particular. When I pulled people over for some violation, I always smiled and greeted them like I was glad to see them. They seldom returned the courtesy.

Nervous drivers always started talking right away. There was a reason they were speeding: their child was very sick at home or something was wrong with their speedometer (they were going to get it fixed). Sometimes their grandmother was dying. Teenagers often talked of homicidal parents at home: "You don't understand," they would beg and then whine, "if I take home another ticket, they will kill me."

I always listened patiently and smiled. But in the end I usually sent them all away with an autographed memory of our roadside visit. It was the law.

One time I asked a belligerent man to step out of the car so that I could see if he was drunk. He obeyed and opened the door and got out. But when he stood up, I saw a tire wrench in his hand. We were on a highway with cars whizzing by, but in an instant the world had just narrowed down to two people: him and me. He inched toward me, wrench in hand, obviously confident that he could buck the law. I didn't move, didn't yell. Instead, I put my hand on my hip so that he could see how nice a gun handle can look in the Texas sun.

"How's your insurance?" I asked, keeping my voice low and natural as though I were asking about his kinfolk. "Got it paid up?"

He dropped the wrench and put his head down. He knew that the law—and my friend holstered on my hip—had just trumped his mean self.

That's how smooth and quick the law can work. Just slap the power of the badge on a problem and immediately peace and righteousness prevail. If we could just make everybody else do what they are supposed to do, then we could all live the life we want. At least that's what we tell ourselves.

The Texas state trooper's uniform I put on and the gun I saddled on my hip every morning wielded a power that was both real and necessary to keep order in our community.

The badge I wore spoke of a borrowed power, not my own. Every evening when I went home to Syble and my family, I took that symbol of the law off and hung it up in the closet. It did nothing to help my relationship with my wife or our children. It didn't make us closer, didn't teach us how to work out our differences. No officer of the law pulls a gun at his dinner table to make his children eat their peas.

The civil law that protected for the time being had its power in force, do or die. The problem is, of course, that when it comes to our faith, none of us can live up to the law—even if we study and pray. Even if we preach. Even if we work hard to perform. Believe me, I've tried.

## A Journey of Faith

My father was seventeen years old when he felt called to be a pastor. But because of a hurtful experience, he left the church and did not attend again until I was fourteen. That's when he entered college and became a pastor.

When I was little, my parents couldn't agree on where our family should go to church—so we didn't. However, the Boy Scout troop I belonged to was sponsored by a church, and I remember getting up on Sunday mornings, helping my little sister get dressed, and the two of us walking to church together. I was eleven years old at the time.

When my father became a pastor and started Lakeview Baptist Church in Abilene, Texas, I taught the teenage Bible class and even led music until he found a music minister. I was actually good at both. If anyone knew all of God's rules, it was me. But I didn't know God. I had been introduced to a legalistic God and, hard as I tried, I just couldn't make myself love Him. I knew I should. I respected Him. He was, after all, God. He could send me to heaven or hell, and both He and I knew things weren't looking good for me. I knew I could never measure up. I was never going to be the real deal.

I loved to smoke (a Baptist sin), loved to cuss (sin), love to party (sin), loved girls (real sin), and could hold my own in any fight (more sin.) Sometimes my thoughts were wrong and tangled and dirty, and that was sin too. I didn't stand a chance at getting my life together like I was supposed to, so I finally gave up my Christian charade and just lived the way I wanted to.

Syble took the kids to church on her own for twelve years. She knew not to nag or beg me to go with her. When she asked me to please let Jesus come into my life, my answer was always the same: "I already have."

One night I decided to go with Syble and the kids to the midweek church service. As we were making the twenty-six-mile drive home from that service, a realization hit me: I needed Jesus. I slowed the car, slammed my fist on the steering wheel, and yelled out my pain to my wife, "Syb, I'm lost!"

She could have said, "Yeah, tell me about it." But she didn't. And she knew I wasn't talking about the highway we were on.

"I gotta get saved. Now!"

I made a U-turn and drove back to the church, but the lights were out. Though there wasn't one car in the parking lot, Syble had waited too long and endured too much to let the moment pass.

"Olen, let's go to the pastor's house," she said.

Right. But what if they had already gone to bed? I put the car in gear and pushed the speed limit. I had just discovered conviction is stronger than guilt. If repentance meant relief from conviction, I was going to get it tonight.

When the pastor came to the door, I got to my point, quick: "I need to get saved . . . now!"

The pastor invited our family in and took me back to the privacy of a bedroom. It was the most sacred moment of my life. Through prayer, he led me into the throne room of God, and it felt as though the Father and the Son were waiting for me. The prayer over me was simple and to the point: "Jesus, this is Olen. Olen, meet Jesus."

Then I talked to God on my own. Not the pretend kind of religious talk I had used for years in church. In a moment, He had become my Father, and I realized I had waited for this one conversation all my life.

I was thirty years old before I finally understood: I was never going to be good enough. I didn't have to be. That's what the cross was all about: Jesus is good enough for both of us. He had already picked up the tab for my sin.

I didn't know it that night, but the Holy Spirit's wind had just whooshed me up out of the pile of ashes I was buried under and set me on a flight path to my destiny.

## Fake ID

The legalistic route I took to learn I couldn't impress God was a long one. I also learned I couldn't fake anything with Him. He wants a real relationship with us, but legalism always destroys relationship. In Christ's day, He denounced legalism and became an enemy of some of His own Jewish people because He was trying to teach them a new way: relationship with God out of love. The law was meant to lead us to Christ, to help us understand how much we need Him.

Sometimes even after we become believers, we slip back into the old mold of trying to perform (law) and prove that we are worthy (more law). This pattern is a slippery slide into deception. Before we know it, there we are—tied up in a legal knot and trying to limp to our destiny.

I've met a lot of spiritual sounding "kingdom troopers" who feel called to keep the law in and out of the church. You can see them pulling people over, handcuffing them to the "oughts and naughts" in the Bible. I've probably been guilty of it myself in the past. But no more. Judging each other may *sound* spiritual, but doing so always kills real love, real worship, and real unity.

## The Law of Love

The apostle Paul never used the law to describe how a believer should live. Never. Instead he said this: *For in Christ Jesus neither circumcision nor uncircumcision avails anything, but faith working through love* (Galatians 5:6).

If you want to craft a great legacy, don't live by the law. Don't live under the heavy, dark weight of trying to figure out how you can get better. Don't focus on what you could have been or what you should have accomplished by now. Forget about performance, past and present. Instead, focus on relationship with God through Jesus Christ.

And don't demand the people around you perform perfectly. Chances are, they can't. Instead, ask this question, "How can I love better?"

# CHAPTER 7

# *Apply Oil*

When the West Texas oil boom was in full swing, Syble's dad drove an old pickup out to the fields to work every day. But when the oil kept coming and his paychecks got fatter, he bought a new, shiny car for the family to drive around town. He liked Fords, and his brand-new black one sleeked up the country roads around Kermit.

Syble was only fourteen when she got her driver's license through a driver's education program at the local school. And obviously, if you have a license, you need to drive something. She asked the unthinkable, and her dad said yes. She could take the new Ford to school. Kermit High School was only a block and a half from the house, and she hardly needed a new, shiny Ford to get there. But the whole point of everything was that she got to drive a new, shiny Ford.

For one day, Syb was the coolest kid in Kermit. At lunchtime, she piled as many of her friends as she could into her black chariot and drove them to the local Dairy Queen. Nobody got out of the car to eat their hamburgers and drink their Cokes because they were in such a cool car. It was the perfect way for a fourteen-year-old freshman to get established in the super-cool, tight-knit group of Kermit High School.

Everything was perfect until she put the key in the ignition to drive back to the school. Nobody quite knows how the "big bam" happened, though Syble says it could have been the clutch thing. Maybe she should have eased it out slowly before stepping on the gas.

Somehow, the guardrail in front of the space where she'd parked rose up and hit the front of the car. Bam! Just like that. The fender curled back like a frilly curtain on a windy day and settled near the front tire. Syble was now one of the rare Kermit citizens who'd had an accident in the DQ parking lot.

Of course, the party was over. No one said a word on the way back to school or when they got out of the car. It would be Syble, and Syble alone, facing her dad. She cried all the block-and-a-half way home, dreading to see him and dreading for him to see his Ford.

He was in the driveway when she drove up. He saw his Ford, the fender, and his red-eyed daughter.

"Are you all right, Syble?" he asked.

Syble, still crying, shook her head. She braced herself for the inevitable grounding, the shame, and the fact that she would never drive again. Looking at the damage to his new car, he asked, "Anybody hurt?"

"No."

Aaron Rose looked at his daughter, took another look at the redesigned fender on his new Ford, and made his assessment: "Cars can get fixed. Sometimes people can't."

His words made Syble cry even more. When Aaron saw his daughter heaving with great sobs of despair, he decided to end the matter of the "big bam" forever. "Aww, Syble," he said, "I've had a scratch on my eyeball worse than that."

## Grace Relief

Aaron's response to Syble's sorrow, guilt, and shame was the picture

Apply Oil

of grace in action. That's what grace looks like. Relief is what it feels like. Most of us know what we deserve on any given day when our decisions and choices and words create a mess we can't fix. Of course, we should pay for our actions and for all of our sins. But what if we can't?

Then we need grace. God's grace is the gift all of us have to have every day of our lives. What we cry out for is grace: favor we don't and can't earn—it can only be given. John 1:14 says that Jesus is "full of grace." We will never ask God for grace and hear Him say, "No, not today." And Jesus will never tell us that we have used up our supply.

When we receive grace like this, God asks, in return, that we give it freely. Jesus said, *"But I say to you who hear: Love your enemies, do good to those who hate you, bless those who curse you, and pray for those who spitefully use you. To him who strikes you on one cheek, offer the other also. And from him who takes away your cloak, do not withhold your tunic either"* (Luke 6:27–29). This is a picture of radical grace.

That's the kind of grace everybody wants, the kind that pours out kindness to others whether they deserve it or not. Your spouse wants grace, and so do your children and all of your friends. The guy at the dry cleaner and the boss at work and the person who cuts in front of you in traffic—they all need grace.

There's a payoff when you decide to be a giver of grace. Here's how Jesus described it: *"But love your enemies, do good, hoping for nothing in return; and your reward will be great, and you will be sons of the Most High. For He is kind to the unthankful and evil. Therefore be merciful, just as your Father is merciful"* (Luke 6:35–36).

Wait, there's more. When you pour out grace on others, people start heaping grace back on you: *"Judge not, and you shall not be judged. Condemn not, and you shall not be condemned. Forgive, and you will be forgiven. Give, and it will be given to you: good measure, pressed down, shaken together, and running over will be put into your bosom. For with the same measure that you use, it will be measured back to you"* (Luke 6:37–38).

When you give grace and forgiveness and kindness, they will multiply and come right back at you. It has nothing to do with Karma but everything to do with how God has set up His kingdom on earth. When we choose to love and forgive, we are following our Father's heart and Christ's example. We are the children of the Most High (see Luke 6:36).

My father-in-law, Aaron Rose, was a "grace man" who taught me that people love to hang around grace. It's like honey on a stick. When you're hangin' with grace, you're safe from the screen of judgment and criticism. People of grace forgive offenses quickly, understand with compassion, and encourage others—all at the same time. When we receive grace, we're healed, released, and blessed. Who can get enough of grace? Our children cry out for it, our friends need it, and we silently ask for it from other people.

Unless I wake up a perfect man tomorrow morning, I will need grace until the day I die, so my goal is to be a "grace man" who gives it freely. Second Peter 3:18 admonishes us to grow in grace. Growth speaks of a process—gradual, progressive, and consistent—so I don't get discouraged when I blow it. I'm still in the process.

When Syble and I go to Israel, we always pick up some pure virgin olive oil. We can get different blends, some organically grown, picked and bottled by hand. The Israelis use a process where the oil is slowly and gently extracted, keeping the best part of the olive in the oil. The result is so smooth and pure, you can put it on almost anything you eat and make it better.

I see grace like this olive oil: a pure, gently filtered, fine oil. You can anoint most troubled situations in your life with the grace of God that has grown in you, and the result is always going to be healing. When you know the source of grace will never run out, you can be lavish and smear grace on everyone who owes you, everyone who has been rude to you, and everyone who has sinned against you.

Over the years, there have been some who have disagreed with my theology, judged me for some of my decisions, spread rumors about my family, or criticized my marriage. Sometimes beloved family and church members say and do things that hurt. And sometimes, friends prove they aren't really friends. This happens to all of us.

But since I know I'm going to need more grace from everybody I love, I keep cultivating my own crop of grace. I'm more flexible in my relationships than I used to be. When I need to stand up, I do. When I need to bend down, I do. I don't get as hurt any more, don't nurse my wounds as long. I let go of offenses and then oil the situation down with as much forgiveness and love as I can.

Sometimes when I need to put everything in perspective quickly, I quote my father-in-law, Aaron Rose. What he said is not a scripture verse, but it works for me: "I've had a scratch on my eyeball worse than that."

If you want a lasting legacy, leave the small stuff alone. Pour oil on everything else.

# CHAPTER 8
∞

# *Rocks and Roosters*

Admiral, Texas, is one of those true-to-life ghost towns—the kind you see in the movies. The dirt roads have nowhere to go, and there are no buildings, no houses, and no people. The whole place looks desolate and God-forsaken—at least the people who left there thought so. In the 1900s, there were a whopping one hundred people living there. In 1989, only eighteen were left. Now all the rest are in the cemetery in the used-to-be town. The only thing that moves in Admiral is the Texas tumbleweed that rolls between the headstones.

I made the trip to this west Texas town with my father-in-law, Aaron Rose. At age eighty-five, he wanted to visit his childhood roots and see if he could still remember where his mom's and dad's graves were located. It's the kind of trip old people make when the past and the present are getting ready to merge into eternity.

As we walked together down deserted dirt roads, Aaron pointed out the past: where the old post office used to be, what the general store was like, and where he went to school. We looked at phantom buildings, long gone.

When we got to the cemetery, Aaron found his parents, Alexander and Lucy. Their lives had never interested me much before. But that day in Admiral, it dawned on me that those roots were not only Aaron's but also my great-grandchildren's. I listened up.

Lucy and Alexander had nine boys and four girls. Lucy died bringing son number ten into the world. That same day, Alexander went out into the pasture, found a sandstone rock, and took it home so that he could make her headstone. He had to use a sharp nail to carve her name on the stone, but that wasn't the hardest part of what he did. Alexander couldn't read and couldn't write. Somebody had to print big letters so that he could copy Lucy's name.

Every afternoon Alexander sat under a tree, crying and carving out the strange-looking lines and curves that spelled the name of his beloved Lucy. He had lost the love of his life, and he never remarried.

Looking at the crude headstone that day made me feel like I'd just met Alexander. Whatever else he was, the grooved-out rock spoke of a man who was both tenacious and tender. He loved his wife and family until the end—raised ten children on his own. His home is now long gone. His church burned to the ground. His town is but a memory. Yet Lucy's stone is still standing, an eternal testament to the legacy of Alexander.

As Aaron and I left the cemetery that day, I thought we were through with my lineage lesson for the day. But no, Aaron had one more thing to show me. He wanted to walk down Main Street, and as we did, he reconstructed his mind's image of the past for me. One by one, he named the buildings that used to be there. But then he stopped abruptly.

"Right here is where I did the worst thing I ever did in my life," he said. The words came out slow and somber, and I knew it was not going to be a happy story. I didn't want to hear it, and I was relieved Syble and her mom weren't there with us for the confessional.

More than any other man in my life, Aaron Rose had always been my hero. He was a dad, mentor, friend, and teacher—all rolled into one. He was a godly man and a poet, contemplative and spiritual. He laughed and loved like nobody I'd ever met. I had always wanted to be just like Aaron Rose.

So no, I didn't want to hear any of his sins that day. And God knows that town didn't need another ghost story.

"Aaron, you don't have to tell me anything," I said, almost pleading. But he did anyway.

"Well, right here was a house where a widow lady lived, and she had two daughters."

I remember thinking, here it comes; both of us are going to be sorry he's doing this. I wanted to get out of Admiral just like all the other smart people in the town had already done. But Aaron kept talking.

"She had one rooster. Every day on my way to school, that rooster attacked me. He clawed my legs and pecked at my arms. Every day. One day I picked up a stick and beat him to death. Hid the body. Never told anybody."

Aaron paused, waiting for my reaction. I thought maybe there was another punch line—but no. He was talking about a rooster.

"That's it, Aaron? That's the worst thing you've ever done?"

"Olen, God said the way we show our love for Him is to take care of the widows and orphans. That rooster was the woman's livelihood. She sold the eggs it provided. I took away the income of a single parent raising her daughters."

Aaron's eyes glistened with tears. I was moved as I looked at that eighty-five-year-old man with the pure, gentle spirit. A man who still grieved the memory of making life harder for someone else. It was the first time I had felt the pure conviction of God through the purity of someone else's life.

It was then that I first understood what a tender conscience looked like. I thought back over the sins I'd committed, all of them worse than killing a rooster. I wanted Aaron's tender conscience, and there was only one way to get it.

"If that's the worst sin you've ever committed, pray for me," I said. He knew I was serious.

Aaron prayed for me, and at the same time I earnestly asked God to give me the kind of heart Aaron had. I was a believer, a preacher. But I wanted more of a tender-to-the-touch heart—just like Aaron's.

## A Heart of Flesh

God talks about this kind of heart in Ezekiel 36:26: *"I will give you a new heart and put a new spirit within you; I will take the heart of stone out of your flesh and give you a heart of flesh."* This heart of flesh that God gives us is no small thing. In fact, a tender, sensitive heart, or conscience, is one of the greatest gifts we can receive , and it comes only from God. Even when we don't know what to do in a situation, a tender heart toward God will guide us in the right direction. "What do You want me to do?" and "Lord, I want to please You *now*," is the language of a heart that is well connected to its Creator.

A stone-cold heart can't feel the weight of its sin. It's like nerve endings in our body that calcify. Signals are sent from the brain to say something's not working, and if we're healthy, we will feel the pain. We know to be alarmed if an arm goes numb or a big toe loses its feeling. But we are not always aware when our conscience starts to harden. Small compromises and tiny little lies we tell ourselves and others don't always seem like a big deal. The loss of integrity doesn't happen overnight; it usually diminishes slowly over time. Paul says it like this in 1Timothy 4:2: *speaking lies in hypocrisy, having their own conscience seared with a hot iron.* The Holy Spirit speaks through our conscience even when we don't yet know Him. We are created with an internal GPS that always navigates us toward God. We have to keep turning it off to get it to quit working.

Without the Holy Spirit's work in our heart, we can develop a shell so hard that teaching in any form is repugnant (we don't need it, it's for other people), love is hard to find (we can't trust anybody anymore), and isolation is normal (only hypocrites go to church).

With a stony heart, we can hurt people and never know it. Movies with graphic sex and violence don't bother us so much anymore. Criticizing and judging feel normal. Anger and rage feel justified. All the spiritual senses are skewed and off balance. When there is no sensitivity to sin, there is also no alert to repentance or change.

God's gift of a heart of flesh comes with a tenderness and clear conscience. God doesn't need to use a hammer to get our attention. A gentle pinprick alerts us that something is wrong and needs to be adjusted. Paul said it like this: *For our boasting is this: the testimony of our conscience that we conducted ourselves in the world in simplicity and godly sincerity, not with fleshly wisdom but by the grace of God, and more abundantly toward you* (2 Corinthians 1:12).

If we can feel the Holy Spirit's nudge, we can stop damaging words from coming out of our mouth before they hurt and wound. We can sense when we've grieved God though our actions. We know when we need to apologize.

I've discovered (maybe a little late in the game) that I don't need to give my opinion so often. I don't judge as quickly now. I keep asking God to keep my heart and spirit tender. I want to feel the Holy Spirit's presence and respond quickly to His voice.

The rooster buried on the side of the road and the "I love Lucy" rock in Admiral's cemetery have made an impact on me—and on my children after me. Both stories speak of men with tender hearts who loved like crazy till the end. I'm proud I got grafted into their bloodline.

We may not be Abraham, Isaac, and Jacob, but we are Alexander, Aaron, and Olen.

# CHAPTER 9

∾

# *Intimate Encounters*

When I knew—really knew—I was called to ministry, I realized I had one major problem: I didn't enjoy God. I was bored with the God of my youth. He was too high, too holy, too far away. But then I thought, maybe the problem was with me. Maybe I was too carnal, too cold, too calloused of soul to relate to God.

Either way, I decided I was going to be aggressive and try to get to know Him. Out there somewhere was a supernatural God—the kind who could take my breath away with His presence and power.

My problem was obvious to me: I needed more knowledge. So I enrolled in Southwestern Baptist Theological Seminary, the second largest seminary in the United States. I studied in the mornings and worked as a youth pastor in the afternoons. At night I worked as a security guard to support my family.

I learned theology and eschatology. I could correctly pronounce "hermeneutics." I could prepare either an exegetical sermon or a topical one. I could read *Strong's Concordance* and study ancient maps of the Middle East to track the historic missions of the apostle Paul.

But God and I still weren't connecting. I had a lot more knowledge about Him, but my prayer times did nothing for me. As far as I could tell, God wasn't loving those times either. I was putting in a lot of work to be a professional pastor, but He wasn't showing up, and that frustrated me. More than anything, I wanted intimacy with God, a back and forth sharing. If we couldn't talk, this relationship was going to be a long haul for both of us.

And if God wasn't in a theology class, then where was He?

There was one thing left for me to do, and that was to go after Him some more. So, every day when I left the seminary, I went to the children's department of the church and locked myself in a small room. I left my heavy theology books and homework assignments alone. In the morning, I was Olen, theology student and pastor-in-process. In the afternoon, I was God's child, listening for and learning the sound of my heavenly Father's voice.

I started by reading the book of Genesis and then writing down my notes and thoughts. What does this mean, Lord? Why did you say that? What does this have to do with me, now? They were simple questions, but crucial to my goal of knowing Him. If I didn't ask simple questions, I wouldn't learn, I wouldn't hear.

The small Sunday-school room where I locked myself for prayer and solitude was a stark contrast to the hallowed halls of the seminary, but it was appropriate for my need. There I learned Matthew 18:3 anew: *"Assuredly, I say to you, unless you are converted and become as little children, you will by no means enter the kingdom of heaven."*

## Pray Honest

I was sure God was pleased that I was pursuing my call and studying His Word at seminary. But I knew He was also waiting for me to drop my religious persona and be the "real me" with Him.

Like a child, I began to open my heart to God. I left the fluffy prayers alone. I realized the Holy Spirit already knew everything anyway. Why would I try to outwit Him by using spiritual phrases that didn't do anything for me—or Him?

Instead of using religious platitudes, I told God how I felt. If I was angry, I told Him why. If I was hurting, I told Him where. And when I couldn't forgive quickly, I told Him that too. "I'm not ready to forgive," I'd say, and then wait to see if He got angry. He didn't. Instead, He was compassionate and kind—and He waited for me.

I learned something Adam and Eve didn't get: it doesn't pay to hide from God; it's better to go out before Him, naked and vulnerable. I learned God was not as interested in my sin as He was in having a relationship with me. Once I understood this basic attribute of God, it changed everything for me. Without both of us thinking of my sin all the time, there was hope. God and I could connect.

I found out two things during this time. First, God listens: *He who planted the ear, shall He not hear?* (Psalm 94:9). Second, I discovered God teaches me how to listen to Him: *Sacrifice and offering You did not desire; my ears you have opened* (Psalm 40:6).

According to Ecclesiastes 3:11, God has set eternity in our hearts. It's His own homing device inside us, the spiritual chip He embedded in us from the beginning.

I found that just like I don't want a "robot God" who can only be found by pressing the right liturgical buttons and formulas, He doesn't want a "robot son" who fakes his worship or edits his prayers. No one told me this. But I found out anyway. God loves being with me. I love being with Him.

Relationship is everything to God. Everything Jesus did on earth came out of His relationship with His Father. The relationship between the Father and the Son is a picture of what all of us yearn for: intimacy with the God who knows us more than anyone else.

## Pray Your Heart's Desire

All my life I was taught that prayer is a discipline—another thing I should do if I loved God. But this is not so. I found out that prayer is *relationship*. My time alone with God gradually became the best part of my day. My prayers haven't changed much through the years; I still weep out my sorrow. There are times when I empty my frustration onto Him with lots of words. Sometimes I feel so much joy, I think I'm going to burst. Other times I sit quietly, letting my spirit listen. But I always tell Him my heart's desires in the most honest way I know.

The prayers we pray out of duty feel heavy before they get all the way out of our mouth. Sometimes we repeat phrases that sound spiritual but don't come from our spirit. When we have no spiritual passion, or intensity of desire, we seldom connect with the heart of God for the situation at hand. Here is what Jesus said about these empty phrases: *"And when you pray, do not use vain repetitions as the heathen do. For they think that they will be heard for their many words. Therefore do not be like them. For your Father knows the things you have need of before you ask Him"* (Matthew 6:7–8).

When you pray out of the deep desires of your heart, prayer becomes a natural and enjoyable part of your life. It also becomes the foundation for everything you do. Being in the presence of God has nothing to do with a certain church or special sanctuary. Nor is prayer based on whether you've been good that day (we usually need prayer most when we aren't). One time of day is not more spiritual than another.

Jesus prayed often and on all occasions, listening for God's voice, while He was on the earth. His desire to please the Father, mixed with His heart of compassion for people, is what brought heaven's agenda down to earth.

A favorite verse we all love to quote is Mark 11:24: *"Therefore I say to you, whatever things you ask when you pray, believe that you receive them, and you will have them.*" The Greek word translated as *ask* in this sentence is *aiteo,* which means "crave." More than a passing request, Jesus is talking about a yearning so deep inside that sometimes we groan, gasp, or weep it out. We know that when no one else is around, we can pour out our soul without being judged, criticized, or condemned.

Effective prayer is birthed when our spirit connects with the Holy Spirit, who is constantly available for us: *Likewise the Spirit also helps in our weaknesses. For we do not know what we should pray for as we ought, but the Spirit Himself makes intercession for us with groanings which cannot be uttered. Now He who searches the hearts knows what the mind of the Spirit is, because He makes intercession for the saints according to the will of God* (Romans 8:26–27).

If you pray your heart's desire with compassion and fervency, your prayers will never be impotent. And if you know your heart's desire is wrong, ask God to change your heart. You will still be praying the deep desire of your heart to please God.

James says that the prophet Elijah, mentioned in both the Old Testament and the New, was as human as you and I—and that's pretty human. He loved God, but at times he grew lonely or depressed, and battled fear. For a while, he cowered from an evil woman, Jezebel, and let her control his emotions and actions. Still, James 5:17 says that that Elijah was a righteous man who knew not just how to pray but also how to pray fervently.

*Fervent prayer* can be defined as "our deepest desire coming out of a heart that holds nothing back from God." When Elijah prayed that it would rain, he was pleading with God for his heart's desire. He was thirsty. Crops were failing, babies dying. Families were in crises. If everything in our world is cracked-open dry, you and I don't have to be a prophet or a prayer warrior to pray fervently for water.

Water was also exactly what God wanted for His people. He wanted them to call on His name and recognize that He was the original and eternal source of everything. He wanted to provide water, but He also wanted relationship with His people. Elijah craved the very thing God was craving, and aligned himself in a humble partnership with God for the nation through prayer. Even now, generations after Elijah, God has that same fervent heart and desire toward us and our needs. He loves it when we call on Him first and honor His place and power in our lives. Through the prophet Jeremiah He said, *"Call to Me, and I will answer you, and show you great and mighty things, which you do not know"* (Jeremiah 33:3).

## Pray Anyway

Some people say prayer doesn't work. The fact that there are gravesides, broken marriages, and people who need healing proves it, they say. But even though every prayer may not be answered, I believe prayer always connects heaven and earth.

God is *God*. His power spans generations and eternity, and it covers the universe. He lives outside the realm of time and is not limited to our understanding. He does not work through formulas, even when they sound spiritual. You and I don't have to understand everything about God's ways in order to trust Him. I have seen the power of God and the miracles of God change situations—big ones and small ones—too many times to doubt He answers prayer. His wisdom and timing are always perfect.

Sometimes I see the beauty and brilliance of God in unanswered prayers. And yes, of course I'm disappointed when what I asked for from God doesn't happen. But when I don't get the answers I want, I keep seeking Him. I keep knocking, and I keep asking for the next thing.

None of our prayers are ever wasted. Even when we don't get exactly what we want from God, if we pray our heart, we come into an intimacy with God. And this is what we all want: to know Him.

Everything comes out of our intimacy with God. We find out—again and again—that the spirit deep within us wants Him above all else. This thrills the heart of God more than anything. He loves to share His heart with us.

## The Missing Link

When the psalmist David asked God to heal his dying son, God brought the child to Himself anyway. David was fasting and praying when word came that his son had already died. Second Samuel 12:20 is a record of how David responded to the news: *So David arose from the ground, washed and anointed himself, and changed his clothes; and he went into the house of the LORD and worshiped. Then he went to his own house; and when he requested, they set food before him, and he ate.*

Worship is often the missing link between prayer and faith. Worship is the posture of the heart that says, "No matter how this situation turns out, You are God and worthy of my praise."

While David was praying for a miracle, his heart was being aligned with God's will in that situation. On his face before God, David's submission was complete. The miracle of prayer is this: when we bow to Him, we come away from the experience like David. We accept the higher plan of God, and the miracle we asked for becomes secondary to understanding the will of God: *"I shall go to him, but he shall not return to me"* (2 Samuel 12:23). Prayer, submission, and worship produce peace and spiritual understanding.

David saw the future even into eternity, so he knew he and his son would be together. Not there and not then, but according to God's timing. Prayer pulls back the curtain of eternity and lets us see that everything is not about the here and now. The main part of who we are and where we'll be is eternity.

Our culture longs to peek into the unknown. Spirit mediums have become popular and almost normal. They are on television and at parties, and they also conduct private consultations. But the only biblical way to maintain connection with eternity is through prayer and worship. The continual revelation of the immovability of God's Word trumps the occult and the spirit transactions of the spiritual underworld. Life, death, and eternity are God's domain. Satan only counterfeits the real.

Intimacy with God comes through prayer and knowing His Word. None of your prayers are wasted. If prayer seems like work to you, ask the Holy Spirit for the intimacy with God you want. Spend time getting to know God. He wants to connect with you even more than you want to connect with Him. And, as in all great relationships, it will worth the time and effort you put into your relationship with God.

# CHAPTER 10

∽

# *Taking Out the Trash*

Not many people know that farmers are really artists. My granddad plowed the dirt with mule teams, but Dad used one of those Oliver 66 green and yellow tractors—the automated version of a dirt-eating armadillo. When Dad dropped seeds into the soil, they were in straight lines with the right amount of space between them. "Look at that, Olen Wayne," he'd beam. "You see those rows? Not a wiggle."

At the supper table we'd ooh and ahh over how sweet the corn was, and we'd tell Dad we had never eaten better green beans. He'd beam like he had handmade them all by himself. We were eating what he had coaxed out of the ground, and I was in awe: Dad could make food out of dirt.

Seeds are powerful, it's true. You can scatter them and something will grow up somewhere, sometime. But if you want a full crop that fills the landscape and goes to market too, you have to be able to see the finished product before you begin. My dad taught me this truth.

Because I saw the natural seed-to-harvest process, I knew whatever crop I wanted in my life, I'd have to work at it. (Without a plan, even a cabbage patch will die.) I knew I'd have to keep a clear picture in my mind of the end product I wanted to produce in my life.

When I first realized I was called to be a pastor, I couldn't figure out how to match my yearning for God with the worldly habits that dominated my actions. I could see a vision of myself as a pastor, but my life at that time wasn't it. I smoked cigarettes even though I knew the addiction was blowing out my lungs. I couldn't quit. I also still battled with lust sometimes. I still got angry. Still had piled-up pain from my childhood.

I needed some one-on-one time with my pastor, and not just the one hour I could schedule at the church office. So I came up with a plan. I asked Syble to cook one of her batches of cornbread and beans so that we could invite Pastor Jack and his wife to dinner. We lived outside town on a three thousand-acre Scout ranch that people loved to come visit. An invitation from us was an offer they couldn't refuse.

After we finished dinner, just before the sun went down, I invited Pastor Jack to go on a walk. I was tentative at first, afraid I would shock him, but I started talking anyway. I needed to dump my garbage—all the piled-up pain and struggles I had been keeping under a lid. I wanted to do more than just quit hurting, I told him. I wanted to be whole and healed at a spirit level. I knew the first step was to be honest with myself, and I wanted a witness—one other person who would listen to my truth—and Pastor Jack was it.

Jack didn't talk much, but when he did, he said things like, "God is big enough to handle that, Olen." Then he let me talk some more. We kept walking. I kept talking. Finally, I opened up the serious stuff, things I had never told Syble or another living soul.

"Olen, the blood of Jesus cleanses you," he told me. "Let it go."

We walked miles around the ranch and kept talking through the night. We didn't know it at the time, but Syble and his wife were doing the same thing back at the house. When the sun came up the next morning, we were still walking and talking. It was the longest confessional of all time. If he ever decides to go that route, Pastor Jack clocked in enough hours in that one night to be a Catholic priest. I, for one, had a new appreciation for his ministry. There was no laying on of hands, no casting out of bad spirits, no supernatural healing. But that marathon confession-walk was one of the most cleansing moments of my life. I felt as light as a feather afterwards—like my spirit had been turned upside down. Doubt, fear, and self-loathing dumped out. Someone else knew who I really was.

Even today, I have friends in my life that help me stay real. I tell them my innermost thoughts and what I'm struggling with. Sometimes, because the people who love me know me so well, they see things about me that I don't. That's when I quit talking and start listening.

## Honest-to-God

The pretending and hiding is what kills us. Lying and faking always require we do some more lying and faking to keep going, to maintain the lie. Sin piles on top of sin because we are afraid of turning over our own dirt and facing the truth about ourselves.

Abraham, the father of our faith, lied to himself, to his wife, Sarah, and to the Egyptian Pharaoh—and thought it was no big deal (see Genesis 12). Lying would just make things easier, a little safer. After all, he was on God's mission, obeying God, leaving everything he had behind. What could be so bad about telling people your good-looking wife was your sister so that they wouldn't kill you?

Abraham's story—and because of it, our story—could have turned out a lot different. But mercifully, God confronted the lie everyone believed to be true. Abraham's situation still turned into a mess: his wife was put in danger, plagues broke out in Pharaoh's house, and Abraham and Sarah were kicked out of Egypt. Most of our own denial of the truth turns out that way too—in a mess. Even when we think our "pretend" lies are innocent, they actually hurt us, other people, and the purpose of the kingdom.

There's a reason we attempt to hide our failures and our weaknesses, acting as if nothing hurts or bothers us when, in reality, we are hurting deeply. Like Abraham, our actions are motivated by fear. Fear is not only the enemy of our faith; fear is also the enemy of truth. Sometimes it's just too overwhelming to face the facts we've wanted to ignore. Most of us are uneasy about turning over our heart's soil because we don't want to see the lies that have taken root there. Digging them out can be a painful process, but it's always worth the healing that comes with it. As James 5:16 says, *Confess your trespasses to one another, and pray for one another, that you may be healed.*

## Stir It Up, Turn It Over

You've probably discovered faith and love and great relationships don't just pop up in your life like a field of wild daises. We all wish they did. But no, we can't manufacture this crop on our own. God supplies the eternal seed. We are the ones who decide how much effort we put into nurturing our own soil, as the book of Proverbs tells us: *Keep your heart with all diligence, for out of it spring the issues of life* (Proverbs 4:23).

If faith is what you're growing in your heart, dig up the rocks and turn the dirt over. It takes time and effort to saturate your heart with God's truth. If you want love to sprout all around you, there's some good, hard work at hand. Sometimes the skies don't rain down the water you need, so you have to find your own. There's mulching and weeding and guarding against insects that devour. Growing faith in the heart is a farmer's work, not for sissies or daydreamers.

When Paul told Timothy to stir up the gift of faith in himself (see 2 Timothy 1:6), Paul was telling Timothy to dig up what had been put in him by the laying on of hands. "You've got faith," he told Timothy, "so start using it. Do something with it. Add to it."

Listen to 2 Peter 1:5–7: *But also for this very reason, giving all diligence, add to your faith virtue, to virtue knowledge, to knowledge self-control, to self-control perseverance, to perseverance godliness, to godliness brotherly kindness, and to brotherly kindness love.* This may sound like a long list, but everything in it is necessary for our success. There are no microwaves in the kingdom of God, no pre-packaged deals we can pick up on our way home from church. We all have to grow our own crop, and it takes focus and urgency. But here's the payoff: *For if these things are yours and abound, you will be neither barren nor unfruitful in the knowledge of our Lord Jesus Christ* (2 Peter 1:8). That's a promise. Stick with the process, and your life will be effective and productive.

## Be Patient, It's a Process

Wholeness and truth go together, and both are a process we yield to. Legacy crops take time. There's a period of time between planting and harvest. Staring at the ground or cussn' out the seed doesn't help. Be patient with yourself and everyone around you even when you don't see the changes you've been hoping for: *Therefore be patient, brethren, until the coming of the Lord. See how the farmer waits for the precious fruit of the earth, waiting patiently for it until it receives the early and latter rain* (James 5:7).

Few of us reach our destinies without mistakes, messes, and regrets. Just like God helped Abraham clean up his mess, He helps us with ours. The good news is that God and Jesus are not sitting in the heavenlies gossiping about us. They are on our side: *Who is he who condemns? It is Christ who died, and furthermore is also risen, who is even at the right hand of God, who also makes intercession for us* (Romans 8:34).

Legacy, our real one, is who we are, not who we wish we could be.

# CHAPTER 11

# *Chasing the Whirlwind*

We don't have majestic mountains or take-your-breath-away seasides in Texas. Our hill country is just that—hills. But we can whip up a spectacular whirlwind or a tornado on our open plains that is something to behold. Gusting, whirling winds, sometimes up to two hundred miles an hour, rotate inside a giant dust cone. These visible blasts of power remind me of another world and another power.

Even as a child, whirlwinds made me think of God. None of us can contain a whirlwind; we can only watch it. One time God hid inside one when He spoke to Job. Another time He swooped up the prophet Elijah and took him straight to heaven through a whirlwind. Whirlwinds prove God has the power to whittle everything down to size—even the opinions of people. Nobody brags about his own power or wisdom when the earth rumbles. No one can find the control button to stop it.

I yearned to know a supernatural God who connects heaven and earth with such power that it makes foundations shake and rocks dance. My traditional church background was solid in teaching faith for salvation. I believed with all my heart God wanted to demonstrate His love and power in the earth. But surely, I thought, there must be more.

I studied for my degree in theology, but in our prestigious seminary, we labeled anyone who believed in the supernatural as "weird." The miracles in the New Testament were a study in history and theology; they were not practical and not for today. Everyone I knew agreed on this.

For instance, the idea of speaking in tongues was an outrageous joke most of the time (shunda-whaaat?). The concept only became dangerous if we believed or practiced it. No problem there. I didn't believe.

I was in my last semester of my seminary education, and I knew I was on "the home stretch." I was within months of being Rev. Olen Griffing, and I said, "Yahoo and amen!" I was ready to get out of the classroom and do some real, live pastoring.

One morning, the president of our seminary announced that Dr. McGregor, professor of New Testament studies, would speak on "The Modern Phenomenon of Glossolalia." It was 1972, a time when the subject of the Holy Spirit and speaking in tongues, deemed to be a Pentecostal experience, was being hotly debated within all denominations. The topic in question came from the book of Acts: *When the Day of Pentecost had fully come, they were all with one accord in one place. And suddenly there came a sound from heaven, as of a rushing mighty wind, and it filled the whole house where they were sitting. Then there appeared to them divided tongues, as of fire, and one sat upon each of them. And they were all filled with the Holy Spirit and began to speak with other tongues, as the Spirit gave them utterance* (Acts 2:2–4).

The title and subject of Dr. McGregor's message insured that no one would miss the class in the main auditorium. He had been selected to address this modern-day phenomenon from a biblical perspective.

Those of us who had gathered in the auditorium that day were worshiping the Lord, as was our practice. The last song we sang was "There's a Sweet, Sweet Spirit." When Dr. McGregor walked up to the pulpit, he didn't say a word. He was authoritative and peaceful, not at all nervous. So why wasn't he speaking? He had the full attention of a thousand student pastors and evangelists. We leaned forward.

The professor began what we later referred to as his "show and tell" presentation with a nod, signaling the sound booth to begin playing a recording. Coming from the speakers on each side of the chapel, we heard the recorded voice of a woman speaking in a foreign language. Only it was not a language any of us had heard before; we instantly knew she was speaking in tongues. All one thousand of us were riveted in our seats.

I'd never heard anyone speak in tongues before in my life. I'd only heard people talking about it. But this new sound was like honey to me. It poured over me—into my ears and all over my spirit. When the strange-sounding words ceased, no one moved. No one talked. Not even Dr. McGregor. The chapel was engulfed in quiet. When the professor finally started to speak, he had our full attention. He told us the message we had just heard was recorded the night before in a home-group meeting.

For the next hour, he led us through a New Testament study, establishing a scriptural foundation that, in my mind, validated the experience. (Delete this small sentence. We were ministers-in-training and leaders. All of us had opinions, and most of us were verbal about them—after all, we were preachers. We expressed our ideas about the pros and cons of speaking in tongues and asked deep theological questions. Is it new? Is it in the Bible? Is it demonic or schizo? Will it go away?

As it turned out, Dr. McGregor neither publicly endorsed nor condemned the experience. Instead, he concluded by saying each one of us would have to determine our own answers.

## In Search of the Supernatural

I knew for sure I wanted more of God and a relationship with a *supernatural* God. "So, yes," I told God one night, "I'm in. If there is a line to sign up for more of You, I want to be in it."

I could almost feel the whirlwind.

The next day, I slipped out of my evangelism class and left my briefcase by my chair so they'd not count me absent. I went down to the basement, found an empty prayer room, and stretched out on the floor. The musty-smelling burgundy carpet was an altar, and I was the offering on top of it. "All of me," I told God.

"Here I am, Holy Spirit," I talked to Him directly. "I didn't know You were a *person* of the Trinity. I thought You were only an influence. But now I know. Jesus, please baptize me with the Holy Spirit."

I felt the tangible presence of God, which I can now only describe as wave of love that consumed every fiber of my being: spirit, soul, and body. For thirty minutes all I could do was lie in a holy quiet on the floor. No one would know of my personal "Holy Spirit Class," which was fine by me. I just wanted to know if the Holy Spirit was real—and I'd found out through a divine experience, which was mine alone to treasure, that He was, indeed, very real.

When we ask the Lord to baptize us with His Spirit, that's just what He does: *"If you then, being evil, know how to give good gifts to your children, how much more will your heavenly Father give the Holy Spirit to those who ask Him!"* (Luke 11:13).

After leaving the prayer room, I climbed the stairs to the now-empty classroom to retrieve my briefcase. Then I went directly to my car to make the thirty-minute drive to my church in Arlington, where I served as the youth pastor. When I arrived at the church, I parked my car, grabbed my briefcase, and went directly to the front office where the pastor was talking with the church secretary. Before I could say a word, he met me with a question: "What's this stuff I hear going on at the seminary?"

I couldn't believe it. It had been less than an hour since I'd had my own experience with the Holy Spirit and only a little more than twenty-four hours since Dr. McGregor had delivered his controversial message to our seminary. Obviously, someone had called my pastor and told him about the latter.

I played dumb, like I didn't know what he was talking about.

"I don't go for this holy roller and tongues stuff," he told me, and then he turned and walked away.

I nodded and kept my cool. He was the boss. No tongues. That was not a problem for me, especially since tongues had not been a part of my experience with God that morning.

After the pastor was out of hearing range, the church secretary looked at me and asked, "What is tongues?"

I tried to remember Dr. McGregor's words so that I could repeat the explanation correctly. "It's a language of men and angels," I said with my best seminarian authority.

"I know," she said. "But what does it sound like?"

I remembered the recording we'd heard in the chapel and thought it might be helpful to speak words that sounded like the woman praying in tongues. I opened my mouth with the intent of demonstrating what I had heard that morning, but that is not what came out of my mouth. Perhaps the best way to describe it is that, all at once I felt as if a dam had broken inside me and this light, glorious language rolled out; it was a language I didn't know and most certainly had never spoken before.

I didn't want this glorious, exhilarating experience to end, but it was neither the time nor the place for it, so after a few moments, I stopped speaking.

The secretary was speechless, her eyes wide in disbelief. Mine were too. We both registered the same fact at the same time: that's what tongues sound like. I picked up my briefcase and walked calmly away, like what I'd just done was the most natural thing in the world.

When I got to my office, I shut the door and hit the floor on my knees. "O God!" was all I could say. "O God!" I had the gift of tongues. I had asked for the Holy Spirit and never thought much about the tongues part. But now it was obvious; I spoke in tongues. The secretary and I had just heard it.

Despite the fact that I'd just had a supernatural encounter with a supernatural God, I felt no great gratitude, no holy anointing. All I felt was an overwhelming knowledge that I had just lost my job as youth pastor. I knew I wouldn't be able to explain this to Syble or anyone else. I saw my future, and it was not good. I'd be ostracized, made fun of, called names. All of this with graduation so close.

But I shouldn't have worried. Although the church secretary was obviously stunned by my earlier outburst, she never told anyone. She and I shared a secret, and neither of us spoke of it again. Life turned out to be normal after all. I was convinced my personal prayer language would be just that, personal. If I never mentioned it, who would know or possibly care?

Syble, that's who.

One morning she sat me down on the sofa and said, "We need to talk." I couldn't think of a reason why, but then again, I never knew why we had to have talks. I let her begin.

"You can tell me, Olen," was how she began the conversation.

"Tell you what?"

"Something's up," she said. "You're being too nice. Smiling all the time . . . like you're up to something."

"You're crazy," I told her. How could she think I was up to something? I had never been so close to God in my life.

"I can tell," she kept going. "You're happy and singing and smiling all the time. What's up?"

I figured she wouldn't get it either, but I decided to tell her anyway. "I've been baptized in the Holy Spirit."

She nodded her head like what I said was no big deal. But I didn't want any secrets with Syb, so I kept talking. "And I also speak in tongues now."

The conversation just got done. Syble's back stiffened straight, and her mouth shut in a thin, tight line. The look in her eyes said more than words: she thought I'd gone to the slap-dab-crazy side.

I knew from experience, when it came to our marriage, the best thing I could do was keep my mouth shut and let God handle the matter of the Holy Spirit. After all, Syble had never tried to "fix" me in the early days of our marriage when I'd behaved so selfishly. Instead, she had prayed and then lived out her faith in front of me. That was the same approach I took with her concerning the Holy Spirit. I never mentioned it again after that night.

Over the next three years, the Holy Spirit gently wooed Syble. Several of the women in our church had been filled with the Holy Spirit, and they were not shy about talking about it. But the most significant impact was made when Vinita Copeland, mother of Kenneth Copeland, spoke to our women's prayer group about the Holy Spirit. Armed with biblical truth and inspired by the testimonies of others, Syble knelt in our family room and asked the Lord to baptize her in the Holy Spirit. That's just what He did, and at that moment she spoke in tongues for the first time.

Connecting with the supernatural is meant to be a natural part of the Christian experience. But the decision is ours. We can sit on the sidelines and live out a "milk toast" Christianity, or we can grab hold of the whirlwind and experience all Jesus has provided for us. I've experienced both, and I highly recommend the latter.

When I tell people I love Jesus today more than ever, they don't always get it. If I say the Father seems more accessible and lovely to me than ever before, some may think I'm bragging. All I know is, for now, I want to pray more than I want to argue and debate.

Hmmm . . . come to think of it, this could be the Holy Spirit too.

# CHAPTER 12

# *Trumping Dracula*

One day I came across a teaching by R. A. Torrey, a contemporary of D. L. Moody. I found Torrey's book *The Person and Work of the Holy Spirit* at a used bookstore in Fort Worth, and I devoured the study book like it was a personal journal.

Rev. Torrey introduced the Holy Spirit as a person, an often-misunderstood part of the Holy Trinity. I was beginning to understand. I'd always thought the Holy Spirit was an influence, not a real person of the Trinity. I read how Jesus, after His resurrection, baptized His disciples in the Holy Spirit.

When I received the Holy Spirit, one of the first things I noticed was the joy that came with the experience. At times it splashed up out of my spirit, whether I was having a good day or not.

When I couldn't find words to express what my spirit felt, I remembered I had a new language, and I started using it. The Bible says we are to sing and make melody in our heart to the Lord (see Ephesians 5:19). The great news, I found out firsthand, is that making a melody in your heart and singing it aloud isn't that hard. You don't have to be a composer or even be able to carry a great tune. That's why this kind of song is called the Holy Spirit's song or, as some refer to it, singing in the Spirit.

Contrary to what some people think, you don't make these Spirit-inspired words up in your mind. You don't try to figure out what goes with "shunda" or how to rhyme "la-la" at the end of a sentence. Instead, the melody and the song, both the lyrics and the music, come from deep within, where the Spirit of God dwells. God loves and lives in an atmosphere of supernatural music. We join in, that's all.

I've discovered, when I'm singing in the Spirit, the Holy Spirit is focused on the Father and worships Him through me. It's one of the best gifts I've ever had. I keep waiting for it all to wear off like a fad, because it seems so good to me. But after thirty-five years, the gift is still with me. So far, so good.

Today, I still love singing in the Spirit. In fact, it's so effortless that sometimes when I'm out on the golf course, I sing under my breath. When I take a shower or take a walk in nature, I sing. Oftentimes, when I putter around the house or when I'm alone in the car, I sing in the Spirit's language. It's second nature to me now, and even Syble is used to what might sound strange to anyone else.

I never gave this habit of mine a second thought until I was invited to join a team led by a United States congressman and two members of the British parliament for a human-rights mission to what was at the time Soviet Romania.

## A Spirit-led Mission

I flew to New York to meet the other delegates, which included members of the Senate, the House of Representatives, and the Human Rights Caucus, along with the associate director of the White House Liaison Office. The goal of the fact-finding trip was to check out reports of torture, church bulldozing, and persecution among Christians in Romania.

When we were told that for security reasons none of us would be alone, not even in hotels, I knew I had a problem. What if I forgot and sang in my prayer language and freaked out my roommate? If I were going to go down as a weird pastor, I didn't want it to be on a trip with international dignitaries on a joint-government assignment.

I decided to be upfront with my eight-day roommate. I had a one-on-one conversation with him and covered all my bases before we left the States—just in case.

"Listen, I don't know your spiritual beliefs, but sometimes when I'm at home, getting ready for bed or walking around the house, I start singing."

He stared at me, obviously wondering where the conversation was going. I kept talking.

"A lot of times I sing in another language. It's called a heavenly language, or tongues. I just do it naturally, like a habit. I'm not always aware how it sounds to someone else. I don't want you to feel uncomfortable if you hear this, okay?"

"Yeah," he said. "No problem." He was cool and unimpressed.

This could be a long eight days for both of us, I thought to myself. I didn't plan to pray in front of him, but if I forgot and did so anyway, at least we were clear: I wasn't crazy.

We traveled for five days, visiting churches and listening to personal stories of Christians who were suffering imprisonment and torture for their faith. We asked questions and documented the answers. We also took every opportunity to encourage our brothers and sisters who belonged to the same Body of Christ as we did.

I was a part of a highly educated and internationally esteemed delegation, but the real honor for me was to serve Eastern Europe's persecuted people. I saw their lack of religious freedom firsthand; conditions were oppressive and cruel. Injustice showed up on the faces of people everywhere. They looked bone-weary and hungry. Their old, heavy coats were a poignant picture of the cloak of sadness they wore, making everyone—even the young—look old.

Most of us in our group were ready to go home and process the weight of what we'd experienced. We had begun the trip in New York with a charged-up sense of adventure and mission. The stories of injustice, mere rumors before we had come, had turned into stark facts. Statistics printed on paper were now flesh and blood people we had met and hugged and prayed over. These people had changed us with their humility and courage, and had left us with a weighty mandate to do something with our firsthand knowledge of their suffering.

But we still had two days to go, and one more task to complete. We'd heard rumors of a quiet genocide in Transylvania, so we made our way through the mountain ranges of central Romania to get to our destination. We were driving at night, down long, lonely roads, headed for a place most people think of as being associated with Dracula, vampires, and horror movies.

The van stopped in front of our hotel, a centuries-old, castle-like structure that had been around since horse-and-buggy days. The full moon was so bright the large trees actually cast a shadow over the castle. The whole scene was beyond eerie. We learned the real Count Dracula, a man history documents as a cruel and ruthless killer, had stayed there many times. That fact did nothing to help the sense of oppression that had spread through our group. We entered the building, checked in, and then walked quietly through a long corridor, past wooden doors supported by black iron brackets in the form of an X on each one, on the way to our rooms.

## A Holy Spirit Lullaby

My roommate and I found our designated room and walked into what felt more like a cell than a hotel room. Once we figured out how to turn on the lone light bulb hanging from the ceiling, we saw two beds with straw mattresses. Neither of us felt like talking. It was dank and dark and creepy. It was also freezing. After we'd each had our turn in the bathroom, I turned out the light and settled in under the wool blankets that topped my straw mattress. I felt the instant warmth the blankets provided, and it no longer mattered to me if they were clean or not. I just wanted to enjoy the quiet and go to sleep. But then the silence was broken.

"Griff," I heard from the other straw bed, "do it."

"Do what?" I asked.

"Sing that funny stuff."

"Sure," I said.

So I started singing in tongues, filling the eerie darkness with praise. The entire atmosphere changed. It was the whirlwind thing—heaven connecting with earth. Within minutes, it was obvious: God and heaven had trumped earth and hell—and Dracula. God was there, with us, and both of us felt His presence.

You gotta love it. There we were, a powerful delegation from the United States and England, in Transylvania, Romania. We were on a quest to bring justice through legislated laws that would bring Romania's rulers into account. Later, reports would be presented to President Reagan's cabinet, and change would be put into motion. It was a historic moment in all of our lives.

But we were also freezing cold and six thousand miles away from home, freedom, and apple pie. We were sleeping in Dracula's castle with a big X on the outside of our door.

When you think of it, having the Holy Spirit "lullaby" two grown men to sleep under these circumstances and conditions isn't that strange of a miracle.

# CHAPTER 13

# *Holy Hunches*

Part of living in west Texas "Bubba Country" is learning the language. We Texans use words to paint pictures, so if you're not sure of what we're saying, you'll know by the image in your mind. For instance, when I tell you that my little family was happy as a pig in the sunshine—well, you get the picture, right?

Some years ago, I was pastoring my first church in Johnson City, Texas. Our children, Jerri and Mark, were attending the local school, and Syble was loving being a pastor's wife. Finally, everything was coming together for us. We were loved and respected in the community, and we loved the community right back. It was a match made in heaven.

One evening, as I often did, I drove deep into the hill country to be alone with God. Everything was quiet and stress free. Even the jackrabbits, squirrels, possums, and javelinas (small, pig-like mammals) darted in and out of the dry shrubland like good-natured neighbors living in an argue-free zone.

I climbed a small hill and sat down cross-legged on a flat-rock pew, letting my spirit settle down into the peace. The sunset's purple and orange stained-glass prisms splashed across the heavens. I felt like I was in God's church. I loved the holy, quiet moment. The only thing moving were the deer, whose graceful leaps made them appear to be worshiping God in their own special dance. As I watched, I started singing "At the Cross," a hymn I love. I sang all the words and wept out my heart to God in praise and worship. It was just me and God—and neither one of us was worried about how we looked. We just liked being together. I talked to Him; He talked to me.

People often ask, "How do you know when God speaks?" My answer is always the same: "You just know in your knower." The Holy Spirit within us is God connecting us to Himself. I'm sure no one hears God perfectly, 100 percent of the time. We're human. He's God. But He communicates all the time, because He loves to connect.

That is exactly what happened to me another day on that same rocky hill. As I sat in the presence of God, thoughts came up from my spirit and into my mind. The thoughts were authoritative—not of my own daydreaming. In fact, the words were so strange to me that I would never have thought to make them up myself.

"I'm going to move you," I heard from somewhere deep within. I immediately listened up. "I'm going to move you to a large city, to a smaller congregation."

I didn't doubt the words in my mind were from God. I immediately thought of my children, Mark, in the fifth grade, and Jerri, in the eighth grade, hating the idea of being uprooted from their friends and school and community.

"Lord, I don't want to move my family," I said. "But I'll do it. I just have to know it's You."

There were other instructions, and I made note of the details. A delegation of five men would come and ask me to pastor their church. And there would be a mobile home, or homes, involved with the move, though I didn't know exactly how. None of these words sounded exciting or comforting to me. Some of them didn't even make sense. But I was full of joy; God had come out to the hilly rock to meet me. My response was automatic: "Yes, Lord!" I was willing to do anything as long as He was leading. I ran down the hill, got into my car, and drove back to the house to tell Syble.

If she believed me immediately, she didn't show it. I knew for sure she wasn't thrilled. "So you're telling me we're moving, taking the kids out of school, and I'm going to live in a mobile home?" I could almost hear her pleading for us to be a normal pastor's family. But her response was the same as mine, "If it's God, I'll do it."

Two months later, when I walked to the podium to speak in our Baptist church, I noticed five men sitting on the last row of pews. After the service, they waited until everyone had left the building, and then they introduced themselves to Syble and me. They were from Shady Grove Baptist Church in Grand Prairie, Texas, and they wanted a few minutes of our time to talk with us about an important matter.

As it turned out, they wanted to know if I'd consider pastoring their church. They explained the church was in an area that was home to thousands of mobile homes. In fact, some Shady Grove's members owned Mobile Home Parks. Syb and I were both amazed.

I was learning that if we are willing to wait quietly and in full submission, God has ways of confirming His will in our lives. When He speaks to us about future events, we don't have to make them happen, He will. We just have to know when to move.

## Taking a "God Risk"

When God asked Abraham to leave his country, he didn't know where he was going or where he would end up: *By faith Abraham obeyed when he was called to go out to the place which he would receive as an inheritance. And he went out, not knowing where he was going* (Hebrews 11:8). But he took the risk. I didn't know what the journey ahead looked like, but I was going to take the next step.

There are no God-given destinies that don't include taking risks. There are times when we have to fling off fear and the "what ifs" and do what God has told us to do anyway. Nobody can guarantee outcomes. *"The just shall live by his faith,"* Habakkuk 2:4 says.

What if Noah had built the ark and then it hadn't rained? What if Abraham had left everything he loved and then had never had a child? What if Moses had led two million people into the sea and then it hadn't turned into dry land? And what if Peter had stepped out on the water and then drowned in the process? We can criticize Peter, but he had never seen anyone walk on water before. No one else has either. He couldn't Google "how to walk on water."

My point is this: We leave legacies—like Peter's was to us—when we are willing to walk by faith before we know the outcome. Walking by faith always involves risk.

When Peter saw Jesus walking on the water, he immediately wanted to do the same thing. Why not? The idea of touching the top of the waves with his toes must have lit up his imagination. Could he? Dare he? Peter was smart enough to know walking on water wouldn't work unless Jesus told him to do it. He almost begged Jesus: *"Lord, if it's You, command me to come to You on the water"* (Matthew 14:28).

Jesus answered just one word: *"Come."* That was all Peter needed to hear. Because of his faith and his willingness to take a risk, Peter became part of one of the most amazing miracles in the New Testament.

## Have Courage

If you focus on what you look like getting out of the boat, you'll never get out. If you need everyone else to like what you're doing, your limbs will freeze up on you. If you need a guarantee that you won't go down in the waves, you will wait too long to move. But if you can take God risks, you can always be part of the miraculous adventure of God.

Remember, others won't always understand what you're doing or why you're doing it. "Have courage," Jesus told Peter. None of the other disciples watching needed courage, only Peter. Bystanders and critics don't need great faith to do their job. When you're getting ready to experience a miracle, you don't need consultants who don't believe in the supernatural.

Decisions that require risk need faith and courage. You are making something with your life that has never been done before. No one but God can fully define your life.

As for me, I learned that following the will of God in my life always requires taking a risk. I still practice the "faith jump"—the leap I take by faith, into a place I've never been before. Sometimes when I'm facing one of these leaps, I remind myself of God's faithfulness and the adventure we jumped into from our safe nest in Johnson City. We were a little scared, a little excited, as we tried out a brand-new supernatural faith that depended on the voice of God alone. We could never have dreamed what was to follow.

Just before they left town, the five men from the Shady Grove Baptist and I had one more meeting at a local café. We went over the checklist again of what they wanted in a pastor. There would be a vote of the church members. But they said they were sure I was "as good as in." On my side, I wanted to make sure we were on the same page spiritually. "I'm Spirit-filled," I told the group of men. "Any church I lead will be a Spirit-filled church."

"That's great!" They smiled and nodded in agreement. Who's going to disagree with a guy who has just said he's full of the Spirit? And what could go wrong with a Spirit-led church?

All of us sitting at that table thought the future was going to be as peachy as the cobbler we were eating. In reality, we were gnats headed for a hailstorm. (You get the picture, right?)

# CHAPTER 14

∽

# *Fake ID*

The first phase of good relationships is usually great. Both parties think the other one is wonderful, witty, and charming—virtually fault free. Shady Grove Baptist Church and the Griffings enjoyed this kind of honeymoon period for eight months. After we were officially voted in, church attendance shot up. We experienced a sense of unity in our congregation. Old and new members were excited. Local pastors and church leaders welcomed me into their close group of fellowship. Our family felt like we'd just walked in the front door of a life that had been waiting for us. We were home.

But when the new and exciting was over, it was *over*.

Rumors started going around the church that I believed in speaking in tongues. Not that anyone had heard me pray in tongues. My prayer language was still very private and personal. In the pulpit, I never spoke on anything but Baptist theology. Some said my wife and I believed in praying for the sick. I didn't pray for anyone to be healed in our services, and I always baptized new converts according to Baptist tradition.

Why would anyone care how I prayed in private? I viewed the tongues and healing issue as nothing more than a newlywed tiff. "Everyone is getting to know each other," I said. "We will all be stronger after this thing blows over."

Except it didn't blow over. Some members withdrew their membership. Others canceled dinners and dropped Syb and the children from play dates and birthday parties. Both of our children were taunted at school. Fellow ministers avoided me, and I was no longer invited to local pastors' get-togethers. One day when I showed up at a minster's lunch, all the pastors picked up their plates and moved to another table. Despite the growing sense of being distanced from those in our church and community, I still held the belief that everything would eventually turn out okay.

I knew things had turned serious after our daughter, Jerri, walked to the mailbox to get the mail one day. A pickup truck chased her back to the house, where we found her lying on the front porch, crying, scared for her life. We saw the tire tracks on our front lawn. This was no longer a little tiff. It felt as if we'd stepped into an eerie movie that had no plot. I couldn't figure out why so many people hated us.

I went to my office at the church early one Sunday morning, as was my habit, to spend time with God before the service. The lights were off, but I could make out the form of one of our deacons sitting behind my desk, his feet propped on top.

"Are you one of them?" he asked, getting right to the point of his visit.

Before I could answer, he flung a copy of the *Dallas Morning News* at me. It landed on the desk, right near his shoelaces. I picked up the newspaper and read the titillating words intended to rouse drama and hype: Glossolalia. Exorcism. Faith healing.

I scanned the photograph of the people from Beverly Hills Baptist, a large church in Dallas. All of them were worshiping, their hands raised in the air. I didn't know them, but the image moved me deeply. Their eyes were closed, their faces tender with worship. They were obviously unaware that photos were being taken in their house of worship for the purpose of heckling and scoffing.

"I'd like to explain what you've read and seen in this story," I told him. "But I can see you're not interested."

"No, I'm not," he said. "You need to get out of here right now."

"You don't have the authority to tell me that," I calmly replied. "I've never preached anything outside Baptist doctrine, and I've never said anything that would cause disunity in this church. I'm not leaving."

I went ahead and preached my sermon that morning, but the sense of foreboding was tangible. The following night, I was called to a deacons' meeting to discuss the newspaper article. I was asked the same question, again.

"Are you one of them?" they asked.

Instead of answering, I asked a few questions of my own. "Have I sinned?" "Am I being accused of moral failure?" "Do I preach anything besides Baptist doctrine?"

"No. But that's beside the point," they said. "Just answer the question."

"I have been a Baptist all of my life. My father was a Baptist pastor, and I was trained in a Baptist seminary. My wife was born and raised in a Baptist home. My children are baptized as Baptist Christians. If you're looking for Baptist blue blood, cut my vein. It will flow."

Pointing to the newspaper photo of the worshipers at Beverly Hills Baptist, one of the men in attendance again asked, "Are you one of them?"

I'd never personally met any of the people in the photograph. But they had apparently moved past the traditional and into a deeply personal faith. They were not ashamed of their worship and were strong enough to be ostracized because of it. They were practicing one of the great democratic tenets of freedom in our country: freedom of worship. They were being branded as heretics, yet in the process they were opening doors of freedom and worship for generations after them.

"Yeah, I'm one of them," I said.

"Then you have to leave," they said. A church vote would make it official, they told me, adding that they had brought me in and they would take me out.

I remembered the rocky hill in Johnson City, the presence of God, and the voice of God in my spirit. If I told them about it now, it would only add fuel to the fire. Satan loves division, and I am convinced that oftentimes, after he seeds it and walks away, we do the rest. We tend to make big things small and small things big. I didn't want to make that mistake, so I decided to be quiet. I was ready to go; I was ready to stay. I loved the people, I loved to pastor, but maybe this was not the place.

The next scheduled church business meeting was packed with people. I don't recall ever seeing that many people in our building at one time. The deacons were adamant: "This holy-roller pastor has to go!" It didn't matter to them that I'd never even broached the subject of the Holy Spirit in any of my sermons or private conversations with members. Nor did they consider the fact that in the nine months we'd been there, we'd baptized more people than had been baptized since the church was established in 1938.

A motion was made and seconded for me to leave the pulpit. The matter would be decided immediately by a ballot vote. When the ballots were counted that night, the motion was voted down by two-thirds of those in attendance. I was still the pastor of Shady Grove Baptist Church.

The first thing I did was speak to those in attendance that evening. I talked about the importance of maintaining unity, not only in the Body of Christ at large, but in our own church body as well. I thanked those who supported me, and I invited those who voted against me to stay, assuring that each one would be loved and treated just the same.

Even after the congregation voted me in—again—to be their pastor, there was tension in our church. Votes decide, but they also divide. I didn't like the process, but God was doing an update on my identity. Without fully realizing it, I had made a spiritual transition into a new place I had never been before. I wasn't better; I was just in a different place. I didn't have the "new" in me named yet, but the circumstances around me were documenting who I was not.

Thank God, all of us have come a long way since that time when there was so much controversy about the move of the Holy Spirit in our churches. Christian denominations worship together now, perhaps more than any other time in history. Dividing walls of theology and tradition are crumbling as we understand more and more that our enemy is not our fellow believers. Close relationship and true fellowship have little to do with church membership.

Still, when troubles surface in the church, we should not be shocked. Nobody takes a vaccination at the door, assuring immunity against misunderstanding, insecurities, or division. We're all in process, at different stages in our walk with God. God often uses our crises of faith to further the kingdom, even though it doesn't always look like we succeed.

In the painful process of working through difficult relationships within the Body of Christ, He also helps us define ourselves: who we are and sometimes who we're not. When the chips are down and we feel as if we are alone in our corner, the only thing we really know is who we are and what we believe.

## Update Your Personal File

Our patriarch Jacob didn't know who he was for many years of his life. He had two wives and eleven children. He was Isaac's son, Abraham's grandson, and Rebekah's darling boy. As Laban's son-in-law, he was tricked into his identity as Leah's husband. Later, he was known for his great love for Rachael, his second wife. Jacob was wearing everyone's identity but his own.

In the book of Genesis we find a story about the time when four hundred men were coming toward Jacob. Their leader was Jacob's brother, Esau, who hated him, and with good reason. Jacob had tricked Esau out of the most important thing anybody could have: a father's blessing. Jacob had connived, lied, and cheated to get what he wanted. The result was separation, pain, and years of hate and loss for the whole family.

Jacob had run as long and as hard as he could, but now it was pay-up time. The night before the showdown with Esau, a "God angel" came down to visit. Jacob was desperate, so desperate that he refused to let the angel go even though he was sent from heaven. Outrageously, Jacob tried to wrestle his visitor down. A life-and-death crisis will do that to you. Adrenalin mixed with fear and the anticipation of death tend to make you do crazy things—like trying to strong-arm God. This was not a two-step dance shuffle between Jacob and the angel. Jacob actually got his hipbone whacked and was left with a limp. Still, he told the angel he had to have the blessing before he left. Jacob insisted on it and wouldn't let the angel go. The God angel told Jacob something had to be taken care of first. "What is your name?" the angel asked Jacob.

"As if he didn't know," you and I would say. But the last person to ask Jacob his name had been his father, Isaac, and that was about twenty-one years prior. At that time, Jacob told his dad, "I'm Esau."

Who was Jacob—a victim or a momma's boy? A bonafide liar or a cheat-and-runaway son? Even as the angel asked Jacob his name, he was wearing his older brother Esau's blessing. But could it really be Jacob's blessing if he'd stolen it? With Esau's army coming toward him, the question needed a quick answer: who was really blessed, Jacob or Esau? Esau was the wealthy one with his own personal army. His father favored Esau, but now God had to weigh in on whose blessing was whose.

Esau was not that different from most of us. Sometimes we work hard to leave something after us; then we realize we aren't "our work." We parent, but want to be more than "a parent." We love our spouse, but want to be more than "a spouse." We are not "our degree." We are more than all the nametags we wear.

Sooner or later, we need our full identity. Names that other people give us can sometimes leave us with the wrong label. And what we tell people about who we are is not always the truth. Most of the time, coming to understand our full identity is a process. Sometimes we have to lose the props before we understand we've been living with an identity that is not really ours. Sometimes we have to be kicked out, fired, or disenfranchised before we come to understand we were never supposed to belong to everyone else's club.

For Jacob, the moment with the God angel was a roll call, and Jacob had to show up with his real name or not get the blessing.

"What's your name?" the angel asked.

Jacob needed to say it. He couldn't change without first facing the truth. He couldn't get a new name until he acknowledged the old one.

Wrestling down truth was key to Jacob's survival, just as it is key to your survival. Who are you when you're under fire? Who are you when you're all alone? Who are you without the support of family or friends? Who are you once you've been stripped of your false identity?

At last, Jacob gave up his fight. "I'm Jacob. Supplanter. Cheat. Liar."

"No," said the angel. "You're Israel. Son. Authentic. Overcomer."

Finally! Jacob knew who he was, and just in time. True identity gave him both the humility and the authority he needed. As a result of the reconciliation between the two brothers, family communities were connected. Jacob was reunited with loved ones, redeemed from guilt, restored to relationship. He reconnected with his heavenly Father, God, as well as his natural father, Isaac. He returned to the heritage that was rightfully his and took his part in handing down the blessing.

All of Jacob's restoration and redemption resulted from owning and using his right name. Before, there was a blessing from Abraham and a blessing from Isaac, but the blessing of Jacob was missing. Now, he was in his rightful place; the lineage was uninterrupted.

God said to Jacob, *"I am God Almighty. Be fruitful and multiply; a nation and a company of nations shall proceed from you, and kings shall come from your body"* (Genesis 35:11).

We can take a tip from Jacob's file and do something that few of us take the time to do: we can update our identity. We are not our experiences, past or present. They may help form some of the person we are today. But just because we pass through a season of darkness doesn't mean we are not children of light. And just because we may have failed doesn't mean God calls us a failure.

None of us are our mistakes. We are not even our successes. Neither are we what we are going through today, good or bad. No, we are all identified by our heavenly Father who named each of us from the womb: *"The LORD has called Me from the womb; from the matrix of My mother He has made mention of My name"* (Isaiah 49:1).

Wrestle down your authentic identity. To leave a healthy legacy, you have to do the hard work of separating the names you've collected along life's way. Make sure you've done an update on your identity and are using the same name God uses when He calls you out. You'll discover your name is uniquely matched with your call.

Your place in the family of Christ is important because it's the way God intended your blessing be claimed and then handed down after you. The blessing comes down through you. When you were adopted into God's family, you got your father Jacob's blessing, and his father's before him.

When you know your real identity, be bold enough to walk in it. After all, future generations are counting on you to hand down a supernatural legacy.

# CHAPTER 15

∽

# *Ring of Fire*

Ten days after the vote that determined I would remain as Pastor of Shady Grove Baptist Church, the phone rang at 5 a.m., waking me out of a deep sleep. A woman on the other end of the line was shrieking, "Preacher, your church is on fire!"

Syble and I quickly dressed and then jumped in the car and sped to the church. Sure enough, half the building was already in flames. A fire hose was hooked to the fire hydrant, but the water had inadvertently been turned off the night before, so the firefighters had no water to fight the fire.

Darting flames, smoke, and debris were moving and swirling in what looked like an angry fire-dance in the sky. We stood and watched, frozen, mesmerized by the sight. It was painful to watch, yet impossible to turn away.

Syb, who always stood beside me in everything, didn't flinch. Didn't break down. Didn't cry. We were both watching our dreams disintegrate, and there were no words to match the moment.

Church members joined us as they got the news, and we huddled together like we were at some kind of church camp. But this was not a bonfire, and there were no marshmallows. Instead, we were chilled to the bone.

"The Joy of the Lord Is My Strength" is a scripture song we'd learned, and we sang it together. The song was our shield against defeat. There were no answers to the "why" questions, no words for the anguish. Worship was the only appropriate response.

## The Real Battle

It was later determined that the cause of the fire was incendiary chemicals found in five different places; the church fire was an act of arson. While we were trying to grasp the reality of this surreal situation, we were hit with a second crippling blow: our congregation had been disfellowshiped by our governing Baptist association; Shady Grove Baptist Church no longer existed.

We knew we were in a bigger battle than we could have imagined. And it was not with people. Ephesians 6:12 defines the conflict like this: *For we do not wrestle against flesh and blood, but against principalities, against powers, against the rulers of darkness of this age, against spiritual hosts of wickedness in the heavenly places.*

The news of Shady Grove's internal battle over the Holy Spirit had not only touched heaven, but it had obviously hit hell as well. If Satan hated us this much, then the fire alone should have been a clue as to how far-reaching the ministry of this church would be.

But none of our little group singing and worshiping around a church-on-fire could see through the black, smoke-filled heavens. How could we possibly have known the miracles that lay ahead? But God knew.

He already knew that, long after Shady Grove Church was gone, it would be identified with raising up a group of leaders that covered the nations with praise and worship. God knew that a little stream of unconventional worship would trickle through the Dallas-Fort Worth Metroplex and merge with other tributaries and rivers of worship around the United States. A kind of worship—the lifting up and exaltation of God— that would destroy self-made idols, heal wounded emotions, and strengthen families. God knew we would worship our way out of that fire and into the future, and that in the process, we would discover how true "heart worship" reduces everything that is not of God to its rightful value.

If I had been able to see past the smoke that night, I would have known that, even without a denomination to back us, members of our leadership team would begin as embryos in our fellowship and grow into pastors of churches across the globe. I would have seen my spiritual sons in the gospel brought up and equipped at Shady Grove. I would have known they would be like hot coals right off the altar, shot into a world of darkness and despair; that they would go out to pastor churches of their own with the same emphasis on worship and the Word that they had learned at Shady Grove. I would have known that children of our elders and longtime members of Shady Grove Church would go into full-time ministry; that they would still teach, preach and worship the theme song of Jesus and the cross: He is worthy to be praised.

Had I been able to envision things from God's perspective that night, I would have seen Shady Grove Church's ministry to the poor as the vital ministry it still is today. I would have seen warehouses filled with food for the poor in Grand Prairie and across the Metroplex. I would have seen Shady Grove give away cars to needy families, help support students, and take care of single parents and their children.

If I could have seen our future, I would have seen people coming into DFW Airport to conferences and seminars on worship. And from the same airport, I'd have seen our "home-grown" missionaries hop on planes to take the gospel to the nations.

I would have seen pastors from Europe, Israel, Africa, and South America come to Shady Grove Church with their spirits open and thirsty, asking the same question I once asked, "Is there more?" And I would've seen us share our answer: "Yes, there is indeed more." I would have known, out of that night's ash heap, partnership with key national leaders would further the gospel of Jesus Christ in villages we'd never been to and in languages we couldn't speak.

If we could have known all of this in those pre-dawn hours of anguish, we would have included some dancing around the fire in our worship—or maybe even a few war whoops of victory or some hand clapping in pure joy.

But none of us could see anything good in those flames. How often this is true. In times of tragedy, we seldom see beyond the reality of the moment. When we look at and smell death, we seldom say, "Wow! God is doing something wonderful."

But He was. He does. He is.

Have you ever wondered why God doesn't let us see ahead of time the battles we must fight? Why do we have to walk through trying times anyway?

Evidently, faith is very important to God. He has laid out the rules of the battle: *For we walk by faith, not by sight* (2 Corinthians 5:7). He has never promised to lay out our future on a bargaining table while we negotiate with Him. Instead, He asks us to trust Him every step of the way. Rather than provide details of our future, He simply promises everything we need, saying, *"Lo, I am with you always, even to the end of the age"* (Matthew 28:20).

He has already stepped into our future and knows that it is good. He sees the triumph and resurrection of the cross in each one of our lives, and He knows we're winning—even when everything looks the opposite of victory.

## Salted with Fire

If you think the path to your miraculous destiny will be pain free, you might have a few surprises ahead of you. I'm just saying. After all, Jesus said, *"For everyone will be seasoned with fire"* (Mark 9:49). It's a fact of all of our lives: fires come, and afterward we are never the same. Our life has a different smell and taste and aroma. While we may not always relish the battle, we are always thankful for the victory.

None of us choose the fires of testing in our lives. All of us would like to shoo away hardship and pain with the flip of another formula. And it is always hard to imagine that our present crisis is preparing us for something greater and bigger than anything we could have dreamed.

But when part of the old baggage is burned off of us, we are preserved for the long haul. *"You are the salt of the earth,"* Jesus tells us in Matthew 5:13. We flavor the world with our faith. And much of the strong part of faith is shaped in the fire walks.

Sometimes we tell ourselves that if we do the will of God, we won't have problems. Of course, there is no scriptural foundation for this idea, although we wish it were true. That's what Peter thought. He had followed Jesus and had seen the miracles. He knew without a doubt Jesus was the Son of God, that He'd trumped all the demons of hell, death, and the grave.

But when Jesus began to reveal the details of His own future to Peter and the other disciples, they were stunned. Jesus told them He had to go to Jerusalem and suffer many things from the elders and chief priests of the synagogues. He also told them He knew He was going to die.

Peter took Jesus aside in a personal counseling session and rebuked Him. Reading that scripture makes us all cringe a little. Who rebukes the Lord of glory? But Peter did: *Then Peter took Him aside and began to rebuke Him, saying, "Far be it from You, Lord; this shall not happen to You!" But He turned and said to Peter, "Get behind Me, Satan! You are an offense to Me, for you are not mindful of the things of God, but the things of men"* (Matthew 16:22–23).

I don't believe Jesus was referring to Peter *as* Satan. But I do believe He was addressing the satanic spirit, subtle but strong, in Peter's words to Him. Without knowing it, Peter had announced Satan's desire for Jesus. "Forget suffering," he declared over his leader. "Abort the cross plan and think positive." But Jesus called those words evil, satanic. If Jesus had refused the suffering and the cross ahead of Him, the plan of redemption and salvation for all the nations of the earth would never have happened. And you and I would not be talking about supernatural legacies. There would be no hope of living an eternity-centered life, much less leaving the imprint of one behind us.

## Eternal Focus

A clue to success in your life is remembering what Peter completely overlooked: after death, there is always a resurrection. In the same sentence where Jesus talked about his death, He also foretold His resurrection. The two go together: death and resurrection. You and I aren't looking for easy fixes and fast getaways; we're moving toward eternity. Eventually, we have to learn how to walk through trouble's fire to get there.

One thing I now know for sure is this: churches aren't buildings. Buildings can be replaced or moved, or they can burn up in smoke. The real Church is the people who are in love with Christ and need His redemption every single day of their lives. Sometimes people stumble, slip, and slide. But they get up again. You can spot these people easily. Sometimes they still have the smell of smoke on them. They may be covered in ashes, but they sign up for the next seminar anyway. They attend the next prayer meeting. Instead of being destroyed, they become stronger and more flexible than ever.

They look a lot like Peter. Yes, he rebuked Jesus, crazy guy. But Jesus didn't rebuke Peter; He rebuked Satan. Jesus doesn't condemn us when we call ourselves His Church, even when we don't always act or speak in the right way. We're in a battle with the forces of evil, and life can get messy on the battleground. But this is what Jesus told Peter: *"And I also say to you that you are Peter, and on this rock I will build my church, and the gates of Hades shall not prevail against it"* (Matthew 16:18).

A supernatural destiny requires a mindset focused on God's agenda for your life. Yes, it's hard to keep walking when all you see is the death of your dreams and hard work. And no, you don't always walk with full understanding of what's going on in the heavenly dimension. But you're in a battle, and it's not just for yourself. Your bloodline and the generations to come will be affected by whether you give up or go on.

Take the next step out of the ashes and into the unknown. Do it by faith. Worship by faith. Thank God by faith. Keep giving away your life by faith. You'll be surprised at how just one small seed of faith can turn into thousands of lives enlarging the kingdom of God on earth.

Take it from someone who knows about fires: let everything burn up around you, but don't walk off the battlefield. You're standing for your fulfilled destiny. Stay engaged and keep your focus. It's the only way you win.

# CHAPTER 16

∾

# *A Symphony, Not a Solo*

When our dreams went up in smoke, Syble and I discovered a rare find: three couples who did the fire walk with us. The church building was gone, and some of our friends had disappeared in the smoke, but not these three couples. For days after the fire, they brought food (that's how Southern people grieve), talked with us late into the night, and cried and prayed with us.

We met on Friday nights at our house and studied the Bible, talked about what was happening in all our lives, and prayed for each other. Sometimes we put in cassette tapes (you'll find that word *cassette* in the dictionary) and worshiped with recorded music. When we finished, we all went to Pizza Hut, where we ate and talked and laughed until our sides were splitting and our jaws hurting.

Thirty-eight years later, Syble and I still meet with this same group of couples. We still holler at ball games together, fill up hospital waiting rooms during a crisis, and have backyard barbecues. We know when each other's first grandchild came into the world, and now the great-grandchildren too. We learned together that the same babies who light up your world with joy and awe when they are born can later rock your world with their teenage and adult choices. Either way, these precious lives are ours. We laugh, cry, brag, or vent—because we can.

Our group of friends knows about marriages that go through tough times and make it to the finish line anyway. We've learned together that financial woes won't last forever. Nor will life. The key is to hold hands and experience life together. It's easier that way.

The late-night pizza dropped by the wayside (for good reason) long ago. And now our schedules don't ensure we're in town every month, but the eight of us still make it a point to stay connected and committed.

Thirty-eight-year-old friendships are a lot like thirty-eight-year-old marriages: they take work. Sometimes you want to quit, but you don't. Our diverse personalities make up a kind of "United Nations of Friends"—all from different backgrounds and with our own personal family quirks. One of the families raised six children in a two-bedroom mobile home. Another lived with an RV parked in their backyard for vacations. Some in our group are opinionated and talk too much; others barely make a peep in spirited discussions. Some are tight with money, and we pray they don't get our name in the Christmas draw. And some tell too many details in their stories because they have never figured out why God made yawns.

That's okay—no nitpicking allowed. We don't try to change each other, and for good reason. Nothing worthwhile thrives in a judgmental and critical atmosphere, especially friendships. You can either love your friends and let the differences fall by the wayside, or give up the collective memories and legacies you could be making together.

Where godly friendships are concerned, perfection is not part of the deal: that's for people who sit in the church pews and look, well, perfect. We do real life together, and so far none of us have figured out how to make it—or ourselves—look good all the time while we're doing it.

## Divine Connections

Our online friends, those we collect and count, don't take a lot of work. We just have to show up in front of our computer screen every now and then and say hi. They can give us a nudge and we never feel it, and we can touch a keyboard right back to let them know we liked something they said or did. It's a great way to keep in touch. But in the real world, everybody needs the flesh-and-blood version of the online model.

It really doesn't matter how many people you know by name or how many know you by yours. The question is, who's there for you when the doctor gives you a bad report? Who's going to be there at 2 a.m. to listen to your grief? Who fasts and prays with you for the miracle you need to make it through the darkness? If you want a bridge over troubled waters, you have to build it with rock-solid friendships.

There are no easy shortcuts to your destiny; the most secure route to get there is with selected friends who will do the marathon with you. None of us will reach our full purpose in God without the people who come alongside to help us. When you shut yourself off from these people, you also short-circuit your own future; it's like cutting off the blood supply to your own dream.

Sometimes we don't enjoy the gift of connection because we want our friends to be who we need them to be. Most of us enter into new relationships a little needy. We have a concept of who we think the other person is—or should be, or ought to be—for us. But relationships that last are built on the truth of who we really are, not the fantasy version of who we'd like to be. If you don't have to be who I thought you were at the beginning and I don't have to adjust to your idea of who you'd like me to be—well, that's the beginning of a really great friendship.

Ron, one of our friends in the group, had a soft, compassionate heart, but it was encased in a tough-like-leather exterior. On some Sunday mornings, if he hadn't liked what I'd preached, he would call me afterwards to let me know. If a visiting preacher wasn't great, most of our people knew to be courteous and patient. But not Ron. I knew before the service was over I would hear from him. "Olen, what were you thinking?" he'd usually ask. Whenever the church elders announced from the pulpit they had made a decision, I knew I'd hear from my friend. If he'd liked the outcome, in his estimation we'd been wise. If he hadn't liked the outcome, he would hold me accountable: "Olen, I'm done," he'd say. "That was my last Sunday. We're through."

But then the following Friday night would roll around, and he'd show up. We would talk, pray, eat more pizza, and keep going. Years later, I officiated his funeral service and grieved for my good buddy. Today, I still brag about his sons as if they are part mine. All four of them keep changing the world with characters as strong as oak trees and spirits as soft as the soil beneath. They are Ron's legacy, and I'm a life-long shareholder.

Our thirty-eight-year-old-home group has gone the distance because we've found a place in the world where we can kick off our shoes and be who we are. I never expect my friends to act like they're around a pastor. And when they're around me, they don't want to be church members who have to talk about how often they pray. My close friends don't see me as a pastor first. I'm Olen, their friend.

## Divine DNA

Christ built His Church on earth to mirror the relationship He has with the Father: one of perfect unity, perfect joy, and perfect delight. All of us are stamped with this spiritual DNA sample, and we have an innate desire to connect with God and each other at a deep, soul-satisfying level.

We were created to enjoy and delight in our relationships. We have been birthed into God's family. Singing and dancing and joy are our natural, lifelong inheritance. There's a party going on in heaven and

"The Song of the Redeemed" is inside us, here on earth. When we belt out our melody, the heavens dance in recognition.

You and I are part of this song. We don't have to be the whole song of God on the earth; we only need to be one note. We are different from other people in our pitch and tone. Sometimes we go flat, sometimes we stay in the minor key way too long, and sometimes we get off key. But like a great master conductor, the Holy Spirit knows how to correct and then blend our one unique note with the notes of others to create a symphony none of us could pull off by ourselves.

Music is mostly about ear, not voice. You have to tune your ear to listen to the notes of those around you. Being part of a symphony is better than doing your own lifelong solo; the sound and impact is completely different. One is a lone, beautiful sound; the other is blended with such full and profound harmony that it feels like waves rolling in from the ocean. Cymbals and trumpets and drums and violins, pianos and pipe organs, guitars and banjos—we want them all.

If you want to do something great for God, first ask Him this question: What people do I need in my life to help me accomplish this work?

People come and go in our lives, and sometimes we're not aware of the ones God sends our way. We tend to focus on what they look like, who they hang with, and what they believe. We ask what they do and what their title is, which also lets us know a little about their financial status. But when we spend time focusing on these natural issues, it takes longer to get down to the basics of what's important.

At a spirit level, none of these things matter. God knows who we need, when we need them, and He is faithful to send them into our lives. But it's up to us to recognize their unique sound, be willing to blend our notes, and then hold on for dear life. We need those whom God sends to us, and they need us.

## Divine Choices

Choose those in your inner circle of friends wisely. They will make decisions with you and influence you. Hopefully, you will have their back no matter what, and they will have yours.

Listen for the sound of people who understand your heart and who get your vision—or, at least, those who help you define it. Great, lifelong connections seldom mature in a day. But sometimes there's an immediate connection at a spirit level, and you just *know*.

When Elizabeth was pregnant with John the Baptist and she first saw her cousin Mary after she, too, had become pregnant, the Bible says Elizabeth's baby jumped in her womb in recognition. How could Elizabeth possibly have known, as she declared in Luke 1:41, that Mary was going to be "the mother of my Lord"? Because there was an immediate, spirit-level connection, and she just *knew*.

We are acutely aware of our physical bodies and the physical world we live in, but we are more spiritual beings than we are physical. The physical body will eventually pass away, and then all we'll have left is the real us.

As we grow spiritually in God, we learn how to recognize the spirit behind others' words or status or personalities. Spiritual discernment is one of the gifts of the Holy Spirit. It is not the same as intuition, or as knowing through and by the flesh. That's why the Bible says, *Therefore, from now on, we regard no one according to the flesh. Even though we have known Christ according to the flesh, yet now we know Him thus no longer* (2 Corinthians 5:16).

## Blessed Disconnects

Just as musical notes don't always connect in harmony, neither do people. It doesn't mean we—or they—are wrong. None of us can make unity happen. We can only keep our hearts open with love and recognize that we are simply singing a different melody.

We've all known the grief of broken relationships. I've offended many people in my lifetime, sometimes I'm sure without ever knowing it. Sometimes I've struggled with feelings of betrayal and envy and disillusionment. Most of us have. But my heart is always toward unity, even when I can't make it happen. When people walk away, I let them go. If the chaotic sounds of discord have taken over the harmony in a relationship, that's okay too. It's time to bless others and then move on.

We can't make people connect at deep, peaceful levels. But we can keep our hearts available and free of bitterness. We never know when someone will walk back through the door we've chosen to keep open.

There is a cost that comes with great friendships, just like there is a price tag for great marriages and strong families. When we celebrate Holy Communion in church, it is symbolic of one of the things we treasure most in our faith through the cross: Christ Jesus has become our friend and brother. The communion elements, the wine and the bread, symbolize the cost of the gift of relationship with Him.

In the same way, we enter into deep, personal relationships on earth with this symbolism in mind. When we pass the cup to each other, we forgive and release each other. We drink the cup of sorrow and the cup of joy—together. We become each other's broken bread and nourishment. The sacred and divine are at the center of our fellowship; life and courage and hope flow back and forth. God is in flesh form again, this time through us.

If you ask Him, God will give you the friends you need for the journey. As it is written, *He who did not spare His own Son, but delivered Him up for us all, how shall He not with Him also freely give us all things?* (Romans 8:32).

The Holy Spirit will counsel you in your friendships and remind you what is major and what is minor. I've learned from Him that love and forgiveness are major. Staying vulnerable and open after you've been disappointed is major. Being there through thick and thin is major. Realizing you don't know everything about everything is major. Saying you're sorry and forgiving somebody else when they say it to you: that's major.

Everything else is minor.

# CHAPTER 17

# *Which Way to Water?*

Webster describes *disillusion* as "the condition of being disenchanted." In other words, something that used to fill us with hope and vision and desire is gone.

Disillusion is a killer disease. People leave marriages, churches, and teams when disillusion sets in. Great destinies are abandoned. Legacies are left on the ground. Before we know what happened, there we are—lost in the wilderness of what was supposed to be.

It's a miserable place to be. I know; I've been there—and not just once. At one time in my life I was known as "the pastor of the burned-down church" in a community where people (at least some of them) burned down churches. And they never got caught. That did my heart no good. I had no idea people could be so mean. Or could be so mean in church. I missed the days when I was a state trooper, which seemed a lot easier than being a pastor. With a gun and handcuffs on my hip, I could fix about anything that came up.

But when I was a pastor, people were obviously disillusioned with me too, which was a hard pill to swallow. I'd done the best I could. I'd spent hours preparing and praying over my sermons. I had visited the sick, buried the dead, and married couples who were in love. Syble and I had given to the poor and made sure sinners (which turned out to be most of us) were made to feel welcome.

And what did I have to show for it? With no building and no connection to our denomination, I was the pastor of a local church that seemed to me to be on life support. And yet its heart beat on. What once was Shady Grove Baptist Church was now simply Shady Grove Church. In addition to the core group of couples who had stood by us following the fire and being disfellowshiped, there was also a handful of families who believed we could survive on our own.

Still, members leaked out in a trickle, like our door was a broken pipe. I counted anything that moved every Sunday morning, young and old, and still came up with only thirty-nine people. Who could blame them? After the fire, we were meeting in a sheriff's academy. We were the brunt of the community's jokes and ridicule. We looked like a Sunday-school class trying to be a church.

I had no idea that following the will of God would cause us so much pain. We had little money, and when I told Syble God had instructed me to not take any salary from the church for a year, she broke down and cried.

But we made it. We lived through a year of praying in every penny that came in. One week, we had exactly eleven dollars to buy gas and food. Syble was a wreck for the whole week, but we made it—even with my driving to Fort Worth for hospital calls.

We were learning a hands-on version of Philippians 4:11–13: *Not that I speak in regard to need, for I have learned in whatever state I am, to be content: I know how to be abased, and I know how to abound. Everywhere and in all things I have learned both to be full and to be hungry, both to abound and to suffer need. I can do all things through Christ who strengthens me.*

In spite of God's miraculous provision, I had to face the facts: The vision of pastoring a church filled with people who walked in unity, hadn't aged well. I was burned-out, not only around the edges, but also near the center. What in the world was I doing, trying to pastor?

I thought of Marty Potter, my Boy Scout leader when I was eleven years old. I doubted Marty ever knew much about the Holy Spirit. But his training in the natural wilderness paralleled the spiritual wilderness I was in.

Marty had taught us boys everything about surviving in the wilderness: how to know when a rattlesnake was ready to strike; how to make a trap out of a branch; which plants we could eat to survive and which ones would kill us.

He'd taught us that if we were lost in the wilderness, the first thing we had to do was figure out directions by looking at the trees around us. He said, "When you see a tree with leaves growing on the branches, look at it closely. It's got life, and it will help you. Look at the top of the tree. Which way is it leaning? Look for the side that has bigger, healthier branches with more green foliage on it. That side's getting more sun, and it causes the tree to lean toward the south. The north side of the tree is dark because of less sunlight."

Thinking back on these principles made me realize, if I was going to survive spiritually, I had to keep moving. Isolating myself from the church was not the answer. Although it may not have been pretty all the time, the local church was God's idea, not mine. And, of course, the problem was, the church was full of people, not the angelic host.

If people offend you easily, you will always be hurt. The world is full of spiritual fatalities —people who quit because the church experience was not what they thought it was going to be. Hundreds of pastors leave the ministry each month for the same reason. Evidently, none of us measure up to who we thought we'd be—saint or sinner.

115

## A Voice in the Wilderness

John the Baptist survived the wilderness in more ways than one. Nobody in the New Testament was more eccentric than John. He wore camel's-hair clothing, ate locusts, and didn't bother much with what kind of impression he made on people. He knew his call (to introduce Jesus) and had one goal (to magnify the Christ). When his disciples left him to follow Jesus, he wasn't offended. That's how it was supposed to be. After all, John himself said, *"He [Jesus] must increase, but I must decrease"* (John 3:30). A person with that kind of vision would not be easily offended. John was a tough-as-leather, Old Testament-like prophet. Even Jesus said that no one greater than John had been born of woman (see Matthew 11:11, Luke 7:28). That's how much God regarded John.

But when he ended up in a filthy, dank prison, alone and facing a gruesome death, he needed help. Was this the way it was supposed to end? Had he made a mistake? He sent a messenger to Jesus to ask the Lord this question: *"Are You the Coming One, or do we look for another?"* (Matthew 11:3).

It was an honest question, which needed a response. The plan to cut off John's head and serve it up—literally—was already in motion.

John wasn't asking for a Bible study; he knew his theology. While he was baptizing Jesus with awe and trembling, God had spoken from heaven, affirming Jesus as His Son. No, John didn't need a sermon; he wanted a reminder.

Jesus was quick and to the point in His reply: *"Go and tell John the things which you hear and see"* (Matthew 11:14). Miracles were happening exactly as the Scripture had foretold. Hundreds of years before the events of the day, Isaiah had described what would happen when the Messiah came. Now everything was happening just as Isaiah had predicted—and Jesus knew John would get the message. "You're a prophet too," Jesus was saying. "Remember Isaiah? It only looked like the enemy was winning. Don't panic. Everything is happening as planned."

We don't hear Jesus judging John's doubts. There was no criticism or even a veiled "shame on you" in His message. The same is true for us. Even when we're struggling with honest questions about His plan, God is cheering us on. Although there will be times when we struggle with circumstances that bring disillusionment, it doesn't mean our destiny has changed.

At its core, disillusionment is a tool that helps free us from the false beliefs we hold about our life. Most of the grief we bring on ourselves comes from believing something that is not true, either about ourselves, about other people, or about the circumstances we are in. But disillusionment doesn't last forever. John the Baptist walked through disillusionment, picked up his faith, and died a martyr's death. His legacy impacts believers today like an eternal clarion call. The death he didn't see coming intensified his voice to speak through generations and ages, and it is always linked with Jesus Christ. His message is loud and clear: God has a master plan, and you don't know all the details.

Like John the Baptist, we connect our legacy with Jesus' legacy to make a lasting impact on generations to come. But the key question is, is Jesus the Christ? The answer is always the same. Yes, He's the Christ. Yes, eternity has already started. And yes, the call of God on our lives will cost us.

Let's look at the apostle Paul's description of his own ministry:

> *From the Jews five times I received forty stripes minus one. Three times I was beaten with rods; once I was stoned; three times I was shipwrecked; a night and a day I have been in the deep; in journeys often, in perils of waters, in perils of robbers, in perils of my own countrymen, in perils of the Gentiles, in perils in the city, in perils in the wilderness,*

*in perils in the sea, in perils among false brethren; in weariness and toil, in sleeplessness often, in hunger and thirst, in fastings often, in cold and nakedness—besides the other things, what comes upon me daily: my deep concern for all the churches. Who is weak, and I am not weak? Who is made to stumble, and I do not burn with indignation?* (2 Corinthians 11:24–29).

Was Paul complaining? No, he was just being honest. But he also had this to say: *Yet in all these things we are more than conquerors through Him who loved us. For I am persuaded that neither death nor life, nor angels nor principalities nor powers, nor things present nor things to come, nor height nor depth, nor any other created thing, shall be able to separate us from the love of God which is in Christ Jesus our Lord* (Romans 8:37–39).

God will never ask us to do anything without first giving us His presence and peace. The warranty that comes with our faith promises that God will always deal with us in truth. His Spirit hovers, comforts, and cheers us on when we must confront the hard-to-face facts about our families, our ministry, or ourselves.

After we've grieved what we wish had happened (or what we wish had *not* happened), we are freer to run the race ahead. Jesus said, *"And you shall know the truth, and the truth shall make you free"* (John 8:32). When we become disillusioned, we actually gain freedom from false beliefs. Once we drop the illusions, we run faster and lighter.

The Bible is full of great stories of great heroes of our faith. But few of them handed down perfect legacies. We won't either. If we mapped out most of our lives, there would be some zig-zaggy kinds of roads we never expected to take. I learned in kindergarten that it's hard to draw straight perfect lines. A perfect faith that never falters, never fails, never doubts, or never gets discouraged is rare—at least I haven't seen it in my lifetime.

But even when our life gets pockmarked with a few good dents, we can make sure our legacy of faith is durable and useable. Every time we glean the lessons tucked inside the dark times, we grow in strength and grace. Just because we are in a perplexing situation doesn't mean we're in a bad spiritual place with God. Without knowing it, we are oftentimes being groomed for the next open door God has set before us.

# CHAPTER 18

⤬

# *Not Sleepless in Seattle*

Worship is a lot like water. When you don't have it in your life, everything around you is dry and crusty. Our spirits need to connect to God, like we need . . . well . . . water. Without worship, going to church may be a pleasant experience but not necessarily a life-giving one. I discovered this truth when I was thirty-four years old.

I was doing my best to be a pastor, but I felt more like a cowboy with saddle blisters after the rough ride our church had been on. My spirit hadn't seen anything that resembled water in a long time, and my bones were brittle dry, so to speak. I was smart enough to know I needed refreshing, that I needed more of God. What I didn't know was where God's refreshing was and how it would come. When one of my church members offered to pay my way to attend a meeting in Seattle where Judson Cornwall would be speaking on worship, I jumped at the chance. I didn't know a lot about Mr. Cornwall. If he turned out to be a good speaker, great. If not, no problem. Any ticket, any *free* ticket going out of Dodge, was just what I needed.

I was told the services would be at a campground, and I loved all things nature and outdoors. I loved the idea of being around mountains and fresh air, two thousand miles away from all my burdens. I flew to Seattle, checked into a Motel Six, and then drove out to the campgrounds, eager and ready. I arrived early for the first meeting and was surprised to find the place already packed out. Everyone was singing, and most of the attendees had their hands raised in the air, a practice that was still foreign to me, although I'd seen it in the newspaper article about the worshipers at Beverly Hills Baptist Church.

I found an empty seat, and stood with the crowd of attendees as they sang and sang and then sang some more. I was clocking it, and we were getting close to two hours of singing. I wondered, do they always sing this long? The next day's worship service was like the day before, and the following day was just the same. By Wednesday morning, I was done. I loved to sing and I didn't mind standing for two whole hours every now and then, but three days in a row was a bit much too much. I comforted myself by making a promise to both God and myself: If this morning's singing lasts as long as the others, I'm going back to Dallas.

I found a seat by the side entrance—just in case. And sure enough, they sang forever. They wore out every song they knew. But then they got stuck on one song: "We Proclaim the Name of the Lord." They sang it so many times, I memorized it—and then got bored with it. They sang it fast, they sang it slow, they sang it loud, they sang it soft. They even hummed it. I stood and stood, waiting for that song to end. But it didn't. Just when I thought we would sit down and get on with the service, they started the same song up again!

By then, I was sure of one thing: I'm outta here. I told God I was done, and I was sure He felt the same way. A flash of anger propelled me to action. I looked at my watch (to make my point), jerked up my Bible, and took a step toward the aisle. Then, as I would later tell people, it felt like an unseen someone, or something, took hold of my ankles and held my feet in place. I ended up flat on my face.

So much for my grand exit.

I didn't move, didn't try to get up. I knew immediately this was the work of the Holy Spirit. He was strong inside me, and I knew I was in the presence of a supernatural God. I started to weep—strangely enough, not from embarrassment.

As I lay there on the floor—my very being exposed before the God who created the universe, the One who knew me before He formed me in my mother's womb—I suddenly realized just how much anger I'd buried deep in my soul. Anger at the people who had hurt my family, anger at those who had burned the church, anger at the denomination that had rejected me—at people I'd never even met. I also realized I was angry with God. I wanted to scream, "Why, why, *why* did You let all this happen to me?" But I knew that asking why never brings about meaningful change in ourselves or others. I needed to ask *what.* "What do You want me to do, Lord, and what do You want to do in me?"

That's when the words of Jesus recorded in Mark 11:25 came to my mind: *"And whenever you stand praying, if you have anything against anyone, forgive him, that your Father in heaven may also forgive you your trespasses."*

I knew that if I wanted to free myself from all of the pain I'd experienced in my life, I had to be willing to forgive—truly forgive—all those who'd hurt me. As the Holy Spirit brought person after person to my mind, I extended the same forgiveness to each of them that God Himself had extended to me when Jesus carried all my sins to the cross.

I wept like a baby, sobbing out my piled-up pain. I saw my pride, and it was so ugly that I cried some more. I cried out my envy of successful preachers, and realized I'd never acknowledged this envy to myself before. I felt like I was a smoldering pot, with all the dross and dirt bubbling to the top. Anguish gripped my very soul. I just wanted it to stop.

Then, it felt as if God took His hand and just swept all the mess away. In an instant I knew I was clean. The anger, the pain, and the bitterness were all gone; all that remained was peace and a sense of holy serenity. All of a sudden, from somewhere deep within me, I heard these words: *Worship Me, My son. Worship Me.*

I wondered how long I'd been lying there. And what were those people going to think? Surprisingly, I didn't care as much as I thought I would. When I looked up, I saw that nothing had changed. They were all still standing, arms raised and eyes closed, singing that same song.

I stood to my feet, raised my hands in the air, and belted out, "Oh, we proclaim the name of the Lord . . . (God knows that by then I knew all the words). Obviously, it no longer mattered whether I sang a song once or five times. For the first time in my life, I knew the difference between singing a song and worshiping.

Before my spirit connected with the presence of God, the songs we sang over and over felt rote, even ridiculous. But after I experienced the Holy Spirit's presence, my spirit and heart were fully engaged. The words came from my innermost being, proclaiming and honoring the King. I could have sung that song another ten times. That's when I knew I was officially "one of them."

## Forgiveness Is the Key to Freedom

Forgiveness is one of the most important issues we face. As a pastor, I've counseled people throughout the years on the importance of forgiveness. I've held myself accountable too, and have always been quick to forgive whenever someone offended me. But until that night in Seattle, I had never fully experienced the freedom that comes from the kind of forgiveness that is extended under the power of the Holy Spirit.

When we hold unforgiveness in our heart, whether knowingly or unknowingly, it eventually produces a spirit of bitterness in us.

When this spirit is active in our life, it prevents us from experiencing the blessing of God. That's because our view of the Scripture and of others is clouded. And when a spirit of bitterness is active in our life, the last thing we feel like doing is asking God to show us any areas of unforgiveness in our heart.

But how we feel is not the issue. Jesus said we are to forgive others. I've learned that when I cry out to God and ask Him for a work of grace in my heart, He is faithful to give me a supernatural love for the one who has offended me. As I begin to pray for that person, I trust Him to bring about reconciliation in the situation.

I've heard people say that time heals—but it doesn't. In truth, the people we need to forgive probably have an issue with us as well. There are times when we simply need to ask God to bring our paths together so that He can settle the issue. Let me give you an example.

Syble and I had been married for years and our children were no longer little when I realized I had violated my father-in-law by not asking for Syb's hand in marriage. I asked God to set up a time when I could ask Aaron's forgiveness, and that's just what the Lord did. While on a fishing excursion with others, Aaron and I found ourselves completely alone. That's when I spoke to him about what I'd done, and I asked him to forgive me. I'm not sure what anyone else might have thought, had they seen two grown men on a fishing trip crying and hugging each other, but it was certainly a special moment for the two of us.

I realize there are situations in which reconciliation is not in a person's best interest. In cases where there has been physical, emotional, or sexual abuse, reentering a relationship with an abuser would be both foolish and dangerous. And yet we are to forgive. One of the meanings of the word translated as *forgive* in the New Testament is "to send." When we choose to forgive someone who has done unspeakable things to us, we are actually *sending away* the ability of that which was perpetrated against us. In effect, we stop the abuse from causing us further emotional harm.

It has been said that when we choose not to forgive, it's like taking a poison pill and waiting for someone else to die. Forgiveness is not about others; rather, it is a powerful tool God has given us to ensure that we walk in the fullness of His blessings as we worship Him in Spirit and in truth.

## A River Within

Worship, I found out in Seattle, doesn't consist of one fast song and two slow ones before the offering on Sunday morning. Nor is it necessarily one song sung ten times. I found out that when the Holy Spirit connects my spirit to God, He takes up all the space in the room. All I want to do is be in His presence. In an atmosphere where everyone is worshiping, I don't bother with posturing myself, or impressing others. I found out that in true worship, no one cares what I think or even what I look like. Instead, everyone is focused on God and worshiping Him.

My experience in Seattle taught me that worshiping with my spirit is different from worshiping with my mind. The Holy Spirit's presence is life changing.

Jesus said, *"If anyone thirsts, let him come to Me and drink. He who believes in Me, as the Scripture has said, out of his heart will flow rivers of living water"* (John 7: 37–38). I found one such river when I was in Seattle: I discovered it was *within* me. I never knew this before. The experience was so powerful that I named it "The Seattle Experience." It marked a change that impacted my life forever. I discovered I loved worshiping God more than anything else. I had a new passion. I could now see nations bowing down in worship, loving and adoring their Creator.

The Seattle Experience was one of those "never been the same since" moments of my life. I turned into a worshiper. In my personal prayer time, worship overtook my prior focus on self. I no longer focused on how I was feeling, what I wanted, where I hurt. Instead, I practiced looking at Him and telling Him what I loved and appreciated about Him—about His "Godness."

I learned that we can *choose* to worship—we can show up and bend our hearts in reverence. But spiritual worship needs the Holy Spirit's presence. He knows God and all the multi-colored facets of God that we cannot fathom. The Holy Spirit reveals God to us; that's one of His functions. Jesus said, *"However, when He, the Spirit of truth, has come, He will guide you into all truth; for He will not speak on His own authority, but whatever He hears He will speak; and He will tell you things to come"* (John 16:13).

Worship only becomes boring when we don't see anything fresh and wonderful about God. Repeating words that bypass our heart and spirit leaves us the same as when we started. On the other hand, once we experience the presence of God, nothing else satisfies.

The Holy Spirit keeps our relationship with God up-to-date through Spirit-led worship. It is the one thing we do in this life that we will also be doing forever in heaven. We won't gather and pray or listen to sermons in the hereafter, but we will be worshiping God. So I say, let's get good at it. Practice it. Be open to more worship in our life. Let's ask the Holy Spirit to reveal to us more of Jesus and more of the Father.

Here's a tip I learned in Seattle that I'll pass on to you: If you want to have more of the Holy Spirit, you can't be too concerned about what you look like when you worship. That saying we use, "God looks on the heart," turns out to be true.

# CHAPTER 19

## Room at the Table

I fell in love with each of my two children the moment they came out of the womb. I thought I would automatically be a great dad, just because I loved them so much. Now I know different. I'll be learning how to be a better father for the rest of my life.

Both Jerri and Mark have been a constant source of fun and joy—with splashes of pain mixed in for Syble and me. When the kids were growing up, the four of us did everything together. We had fun, lazy Saturday brunches, went to ball games, and made major decisions together as a family.

Sometimes, when the two of them found out what Syble and I were going to be doing on any particular evening, they would cancel plans with their friends and join us. Both Syble and I knew we were blessed. We never coerced, coaxed, or threatened them to obey. (We did, however strongly suggest it. We were also good at letting them know their options up front.)

Anyone who knew us would have described us as a close family with normal problems. But none of us could possibly have foretold the pain and confusion that lay ahead for the Griffing family.

Mark and his wife had been married for five years and were the parents of a beautiful two-year-old daughter, Heather. Syble and I were out of town when we received a call from one of the elders at our church, telling us Mark had disappeared. We canceled our plans and returned immediately. When we talked with our daughter-in-law, we learned the truth. Mark had not simply disappeared; he had chosen to leave his wife and daughter. According to Mark, he was a homosexual.

Syble and I were stunned. We couldn't believe it, so we didn't. This had to be a mistake. He wasn't thinking clearly, that's all. We would fast and pray, and then everything would be all right. He could get counseling. Everything would heal.

Although our church elders walked in love toward us as they offered support and understanding, others didn't. Preachers counseled, friends prayed, enemies laughed, and the community twittered long before the Internet made doing so easy. Everybody came up with their own solutions, but not the right one. Not for Mark, and not for the family.

Syble and I were clearly in unchartered territory, and we had to face the truth. Our dreams for our son were washed away with our tears. My mind raced from one thought to another.

I had to make up for what I had not given my son.

I had to be what I had not been for him. But I didn't know where to begin.

If Mark was gay, then I had failed as a father.

On the other hand, I reasoned, my father hadn't been everything I'd needed or wanted, but I was not gay. Condemnation and guilt spread throughout our family like a pox-filled virus.

Who caused this, and who was accountable?

Did we fail Mark?

Did Mark fail us?

Did anyone fail?

We decided to do the only thing we knew to do as parents: we would show Mark tough love. We would treat him harshly, with the intent of helping him, and all of us, in the long run. How dare he tear up so many lives and not pay the consequences? We had to take a stand for righteousness' sake.

When Thanksgiving Day arrived, the family gathered together just like always—except Mark wasn't there. Syble's table was beautiful, the turkey was cooked perfectly, and the family sat together and made small talk. No one mentioned Mark because we were all afraid we would start crying.

That's when we heard a car pull in the driveway, and we knew it was Mark coming home for Thanksgiving dinner. Syble met him at the door and told him what we had decided: "Mark, we love you." She was weeping out her words. "But we just can't condone your lifestyle. Until you get your life together, we can't pretend everything is like it used to be."

Mark left, shattered. Thanksgiving was over. Syble and I were a mess. In an effort to show tough love, we had just rejected our only son. What was so good about a love like this?

The pain we walked through was deep, cavernous, and unending. Not only had we lost our son, we were losing our daughter-in-law, whom we loved like our own. Heather, our grandbaby-girl, was the light of our life, and now her home was broken. Our daughter, Jerri, was as stunned and grief stricken as Syble and I. Our extended family and the church were confused.

It turned out that our tough-love approach to our son's choices did nothing to bring peace and restoration to our family. We had been so focused on our own pain and turmoil that none of us had really thought about Mark. No one was thinking of his pain, only his guilt. What about his suffering? How long had he been isolated? What was it was like for him to feel the rejection of family, church, and the community he had grown up in—all at one time?

And so I reached out to him. I made a point to take him to lunch on a regular basis. He talked, and I listened. I talked, and he listened. I let him know, although we did not agree with the decisions he was making, we still loved him and he was welcome in our home.

But not only was I Mark's father, I was also a pastor, and I knew I had to deal with the reality of our circumstances from a biblical perspective. The objective was not to be punitive; rather, the purpose was to bring about restoration. One of the elders from our church joined us one day for lunch and showed Mark what the Word of God had to say about his so-called lifestyle. Mark listened to what we had to say. The process didn't make him bitter, but it didn't change his choices either. And that's when things got worse.

Mark went through a reckless period of drug and alcohol use that, combined with his lifestyle choice, nearly killed him. All we could do was walk in love toward him—and pray. There was nothing more we could do; we released our son to God. That's when it happened: not for better, but things got worse again. The story is his to tell, but Mark continued to walk apart from a committed relationship with God.

Recently, I had a conversation with him. "If you really want to walk with God, understand that your sin isn't any different in the eyes of God than any of my sins. If you belong to Jesus Christ, you are no more a homosexual than a man in the moon. You may have a sexual problem, but others have different problems," I told him.

"You know, Dad, I now see that I've identified with my iniquity more than I have identified with Jesus and His forgiveness of my sins," he said. "If had realized what my choices were going to cost me, how it would hurt our family, I never would have done what I did."

Something in my son's heart has changed; he's on the path to a transformed life and so am I.

## The Greatest of These Is Love

Even today, I don't always understand Mark's heart or his choices. But I can't pretend I can live without loving him or having him in my life. And it doesn't matter what he does or doesn't do. He's my son. There will always be a place at the table for him.

Syble and I have apologized to Mark many times for turning him away from our table that Thanksgiving day. His daughter, Heather, is now grown and has her degree in education. She loves God, loves her dad like crazy, and is still one of the people we love most on earth. Mark knows from our actions that we are family and will never walk away—even when his choices break our hearts.

"Do you believe homosexuality is scriptural?" is a valid question I'm often asked, in different forms. My answer is always the same: "I believe in the Bible, completely."

Nothing has ever made me doubt that Scripture is not God's final word on everything. I've staked my life on it. I know a God who is love and kind and just. And no, I don't believe homosexuality is a biblical way to live.

But I also know nothing will ever separate us from the love of Christ. I refuse to be labeled a "gay-basher" or "homophobic." At the end of the day, God and His Word will stand. Loving my son with all my heart does not require me to lay down my faith in what I believe. I am not Mark's judge. I'm his father. Just as I live with my faith decisions, my son lives with his.

If gays aren't welcome at our table—or in our church—perhaps we are missing the point of the gospel we so passionately believe. We are loved, forever. Because of the cross, we are forgiven, over and over. Repentance, for all of us, is a gift of grace, not a form of angry judgment.

Control and coercion, condemnation and criticism—all are pretty weak weapons in any battle of life. Nothing gives life and light except the cross of Christ, working in and through us.

The church often judges the gay community, just as gays often judge the church. Hate, division, and pride become a tangled web where saint and sinner start looking alike: both need God. Both need more of God.

Today I celebrate Mark's life like the gift he is. When we hang out, it is as father and son, not preacher and parishioner. He's a dedicated dad, a gifted man who is sensitive and creative.

I don't have time to judge and criticize, not even—especially not even—my own son. He belongs to his other Father, God, who will be faithful to the end. I want to be a father just like Him.

When God told Abraham to give Him his son, Isaac, He was showing us how to release our own children. The act of father and son walking toward the altar of devastated dreams is the ultimate scene of worship in the Old Testament. God is worthy of our trust. He proved He could handle the pain of both Abraham and Isaac, and He can most certainly handle our pain. "Praise be to God," Abraham was saying through his supernatural act of obedience. "He's worthy of everything I love the most."

Letting go of our children requires rock-solid faith. Believing and loving to the end is a biblical legacy we can live by: *And now abide faith, hope, and love, thee three; but the greatest of these is love* (1 Corinthians 13:13).

I believe all of my children, grandchildren, and great-grandchildren will glorify God. I've made room for them, all of them, at my table. I've also made reservations for all of them at the Wedding Feast of the Lamb. They'll be there. What happens between now and then is not in my control, but I'm taking all my cues from Abraham: I'm going to keep walking, keep loving, and keep worshiping.

Follow Abraham's walk. Release the people you can't change (that's everyone). Parent your children by putting them on the altar. They will be safe there.

# CHAPTER 20

❧

# *The Ancient Art of Humility*

Humility is one of those attributes we all want to develop in our lives, that is, as long as we don't have to be awake to experience the process. It's a lot like taking a sharp knife and cutting off your big toe: you just don't do it unless, of course, you have to.

I learned a lot about humility right after Shady Grove Church went up in flames. For months afterwards, our church got plenty of media attention while the community followed our story. Newspapers interviewed us, splashing our name in headlines across the pages. Most everyone expected what was left of our small congregation to blow away with the ashes, but instead we reshaped our vision and started rebuilding. Instead of focusing on the number of people we had lost and how much money we didn't have, we focused on worship and on knowing and loving God. In six months, attendance had doubled . . . and it continued to grow.

I met other pastors in the Metroplex who, like me, were not connected to one denomination, but embraced them all. It was exciting to be part of their fellowship and to meet new friends. We may have been a minority, but we found out that all over the United States and around the world, believers were becoming more aware of the work and person of the Holy Spirit.

Our church was still coming up out of the ashes, and we quickly learned that rebuilding required sacrifice from all of us. Syble and I sold our two-year-old car so that we could give a much-needed offering to the church's building fund. We found a great deal on a repossessed green Gremlin, a sub-compact car from AMC, and we bought it. Named by *Time* magazine as one of the fifty worst cars of all time, the Gremlin was obviously designed for people who couldn't afford a real car. Small and green might have been okay if we'd been driving a Volkswagen beetle, but in addition to its size and color, the Gremlin was "ugh" too. It was reported that the company's chief stylist drew the first sketch on an airsickness bag while he was flying somewhere. That should have told them something right there.

God was doing great things in our lives, but you'd never know it by the car we drove. In fact, I hated that car and did everything I could to avoid being seen in it. My new pastor friends drove Cadillacs and Lincoln Town Cars—symbols of success. There wasn't one other Gremlin in the group. I knew enough to know the kind of car I drove shouldn't matter to me, but it did. When I met with my peers for lunch, I always parked the green Gremlin as far away as possible so that no one would put the two of us together.

When Syble and I were invited to join these pastors and other ministers to attend a two-day conference at the downtown Hyatt, we felt like we were going on vacation. We'd been through what Texas cowboys called their journey through deep rivers and hundred-degree heat, "hell and high water." We were still living by faith, pinching every penny. We couldn't wait to spend a few days in a luxury hotel.

I had never used the services of a valet before, so I was very happy when a man appeared outside the hotel lobby to drive the Gremlin away. Neither Syb nor I looked back. We hoped no one from our new peer group would see how we'd gotten there.

The hotel was beautiful and the conference was something we had never experienced before. We laughed, cried, worshiped, and prayed together with others of like faith. Being at the conference was as close to heaven as we could get. We had new friends who shared our vision. We belonged.

When the conference was over and it was time to leave, Syb and I carried our bags to the lobby where all our pastor friends were waiting as, one-by-one, their cars were driven to the door. Both of us had the same thought at the same time: somewhere in that line of Cadillacs and Lincolns, that ugly green Gremlin was coming for us.

When I saw a valet heading my way, I tensed up. I prayed my best prayer of faith: "Please, God, let him say he can't find my car. I can get it after everyone's gone." But it was not to be.

"Mr. Griffing," the valet said politely. "Your car wouldn't start and was blocking traffic in the garage, so we're pushing it."

To my horror, I saw two attendants behind him, pushing the car up to where Syble and I were standing. We were both praying for a charismatic miracle—one where the cement drive opened up and quickly swallowed both of us.

Instead, one of the pastors pulled out some cables from the back of his Cadillac and jump-started the green heap of ugly tin and tires. The Gremlin and I had been outed: everyone now knew we belonged to each other.

Syble and I didn't know whether to laugh or cry, but as we drove home that day we saw the absurdity of our attempt to act like "the biggies." We split our sides at the ridiculous picture of our trying to pretend we weren't who we actually were. These were the facts: we lived in a modest house in Grand Prairie, not Dallas; our church was half built, not a megachurch; and we drove an ugly green Gremlin, not a Cadillac.

One thing we knew for sure: humility never goes hand-in-hand with image and ego, pride and dignity. As believers, we know we need humility. We recognize people who have it and those who don't. And most of us know none of us can build and leave great legacies behind us without this grace in our lives. But how do we get humility without a lot of pain? Some people opt to use pre-manufactured "pretend" humility. This requires a lot of sighing and tears, complete with scripture verses slipped into bad conversations.

Most of us recognize this quality in others before we identify it in ourselves, because, well, we need humility. "Look at them!" we huff and puff. But the saying "If you spot it, you got it" usually rings true: what we so clearly see in others is in us too—it's just hidden by our pride. None of us decide we're going to be proud. None of us want to be known as proud. But pride and self-exaltation are default characteristics of our old sin nature, part of the carnal state we fight by the Spirit of Christ. Pride in its ugliest form is what causes us to fight and defend, exalt and divide, grab and defile. Sometimes pride is so subtle that we don't recognize we have aligned ourselves with something ugly and evil.

When opportunities to be humble present themselves, we alone can choose our response. The Bible says, *Therefore humble yourselves under the mighty hand of God, that He may exalt you in due time* (1 Peter 5:6). As a leader, there are times when I cannot explain the private undercurrents of public situations. Humility says to be quiet and let the talkers talk and the scorners scorn. It is hurtful when others judge us on the basis of partial facts. Sometimes our insecurity rises up to do battle.

Sometimes family members go through tough times, and humility's wisdom says to give them plenty of room to let them find their own way. Silence and non-judgmental love require great humility that trusts in God alone. And there are times when the decisions we once thought were right, end up causing grief and frustration for us and everyone around. Humility counsels us to face the fact that we will always encounter difficulties and the emotion and grief they bring. But instead of denying the situation exists, we need to keep moving forward in faith.

## Humility's DNA

Humility, in its original essence, is the spirit of Jesus. There would be no cross, no salvation, no redemption or restoration without the divine humility of God in Jesus Christ: *Let this mind be in you which was also in Christ Jesus, who, being in the form of God, did not consider it robbery to be equal with God, but made Himself of no reputation, taking the form of a bondservant, and coming in the likeness of men. And being found in appearance as a man, He humbled Himself and became obedient to the point of death, even the death of the cross. Therefore God also has highly exalted Him and given Him the name which is above every name* (Philippians 2:5–9).

The Holy Spirit has to cultivate true humility is all of us, and it doesn't usually happen overnight. Choosing humility always goes against our human nature. Our human bent toward pride doesn't naturally choose the low position in anything.

But Jesus didn't grasp at position, although He was the Son of God. He became a servant, although He created all things: thrones, dominions, rulers and authorities (see Colossians 1:16). He emptied Himself, although all the fullness of the God was in Him (see Colossians 1:19). He humbled Himself to become a man, although He was with the Father at the creation of the universe (see Psalm 8). And then He went down lower, to die a sinner's death. He let go of everything—except being the Son of His Father.

## Humility's Covering

There is a rest in letting go of pride and falling into humility's gentle pull. When you choose to take the lower rung of a servant, you are also following the way of Jesus and thus come under His covering of peace: *"Come to Me, all you who labor and are heavy laden, and I will give you rest. Take My yoke upon you and learn from Me, for I am gentle and lowly in heart, and you will find rest for your souls. For My yoke is easy and My burden is light"* (Matthew 11:28–30).

True humility is being who you are without pretense and persona. It is accepting that you may not be as far along in your Christian walk as others around you and that you don't always have the answers. Even when you try, you can't make everything happen according to your heart's desire. That's a humbling reality. Humility is watching someone else run ahead of you in a position or place you thought was yours, and then finding the grace to clap and cheer at their success.

Moses was the most humble man on the face of the earth (see Numbers 12:3). If you read the story of his life, you'll see he had plenty of frustrations, heartaches, and family issues. But his response was always the same: he cried out to the Lord in a spirit of humility, with a constant need for direction and strength. God made sure Moses and the Israelites who followed him had plenty of food and rest, and were well taken care of. Can you imagine him trying to lead those millions of people day and night if he'd had an attitude of pride and arrogance? Moses' humility came from understanding he needed everything from God. God, in return, protected Moses with daily divine guidance, which is one of humility's rewards: *The humble He guides in justice, and the humble He teaches His way* (Psalm 25:9).

## Humility's Wisdom

We don't always like the lessons in humility when they come, but the Holy Spirit will always be faithful to lead us into Christ's humility.

140

Humility is how Jesus completed the will of His Father on earth; He learned obedience by the things he suffered.

True humility asks questions: How can I please the Father? How can I serve my Lord in this situation? What do you want of me, Lord? The obedience that delights to please and serve the Creator bows before Him and says *whatever, however*. It triumphs other people's opinions and our own logic that tells us to stand up for ourselves and make sure we get what we think we deserve.

Peter was doing the logical thing when, the night before Jesus was crucified, he pulled out his sword and whacked off a soldier's ear. That's what you do when people come against your leader and you. Jesus' response was to gently restore the ear and then show Peter what real power and authority looked like: He offered Himself up to the death that was His Father's plan.

## Humility's Reward

Satan has nothing in his bag of tricks that can surpass Christ's humility. He can offer a replica of humility, but it has no power. When we operate under Christ's authority and His covering of humility, we remain in a higher position than all of our enemies from hell. According to Ephesians 1:18, God must open our eyes so that we can see how great the power of Christ working in us is. Verse 21 tells us that power is *far above all principality and power and might and dominion, and every name that is named, not only in this age but also in that which is to come.*

The gentle, tender spirit of humility is both a power and a fragrance. We will always need this supernatural power to overcome the cultural bias against Christ's followers. You were designed to rule and reign with Christ forever. Humility seldom makes you feel as though you're winning. When you take the position to serve or you refuse to respond to an insult, it is unlikely you will experience joy in the moment. However, any time you choose humility, you are prepping yourself for a reward: *"And whoever exalts himself will be humbled, and he who humbles himself will be exalted"* (Matthew 23:12).

That's a promise.

Jesus is proof that those who go up will come down and those who go down will come up: *Therefore God also has highly exalted Him and given Him the name which is above every name, that at the name of Jesus every knee should bow, of those in heaven, and of those on earth, and of those under the earth, and that every tongue should confess that Jesus Christ is Lord, to the glory of God the Father* (Philippians 2:9–11).

That's also a promise.

# CHAPTER 21

# *Fathers and Sons*

I learned the basics of teamwork at age twelve when I was in the Boy Scouts. All thirty of us in Troop 82 knew the drill: slick back your hair, check to see if your fingernails were clean, wear the right socks, and make sure your uniform was ironed. We looked like an army of small soldiers, and I loved it. It was the only place I could go in my life where everyone was treated the same.

My uniform made me feel like I belonged, and it defined who I wanted to be: a Scout who was faithful, honest, and true. The community needed us to serve them, and if we tried, we could be leaders some day. All twelve-year-olds need a vision, and I had one.

"It's not about me" was my Scoutmaster's favorite saying. "It's about *we*." Teams of Scouts survived the dangers of the wilderness together. Teams met goals together. Teams walked over the finish line together. I got the message. Later, when I was awarded the coveted Eagle Scout badge and knew I would always be a leader, I wanted the strength of a team around me.

I understand why businesses and churches are built on a hierarchal system. Everything that we're a part of uses this model of rulership from the top—from the president of the United States on down. It's how our world moves and stays on its hinges. But I've never thought this model was the perfect one for the Church.

## Hierarchy Vs. Relationship

In a hierarchy, everyone is interested in the top position: who's there, how to get there, who's ahead of you and could block you from getting there, who's behind you and could get there quicker than you. Resentment and jealousy seed easily when the only two directions to go in the relationship are up or down.

If you are on a ladder going up, it's not hard to figure out how to relate. Knowing what to say or not say is a no-brainer: don't bite the hand that feeds you. And likewise, if you're the boss and others keep ticking you off, well, who would blame you if they got their pink slip early?

I prefer relational leadership, partly because I'm relational by personality. I love people—love being around them, love hearing their stories, and love telling stories of my own. I've always wanted to connect at a friendship level with almost everyone, including God, my wife, my children and now, my adult grandchildren.

Jesus mirrored the relationship we all long for when He said, *"No longer do I call you servants, for a servant does not know what his master is doing; but I have called you friends, for all things that I heard from My Father I have made known to you"* (John 15:15).

Was there a difference between Jesus and the servants He now called friends? Yes, of course. He was Lord, God of everything. And yet, He ate with them, cried with them, cooked for them, and taught them. But He never lorded his authority over them. Even when Judas betrayed Him with a kiss the night before He was crucified, Jesus still called him friend: *"Friend, why have you come?"*(Matthew 26:50).

When I realized what I wanted more than anything was to pastor a church built on the Word of God and extravagant worship, I had a dilemma: how was I going to find the team I needed? I lived in Grand Prairie, Texas, not Los Angeles. I drove a Gremlin, not a Cadillac. And I pastored what looked more like a small Sunday-school group than a real church.

Networking wasn't a smart option for me, partly because my contact list wasn't top-heavy with influential names or mega-money businessmen. Besides, if my vision was building a house for supernatural worship, it made sense that this kind of church required birthing, not negotiating. If I wanted something to last past the latest spiritual fad, I was going to have to father my own spiritual sons.

Prayer and worship are the womb of spiritual activity. I knew everything worth eternity would come out of being in God's presence and listening to His voice. And just in case He needed my help, I told Him what I was looking for in a team of elders with matching spiritual DNA. I was on the lookout for men with teachable spirits who had the same passion for God and love of people that I had. We would never be on the same page without some basic genes that matched and could be reproduced.

God answered my prayer. He brought me the team I needed, even though each member was in embryo form. One by one, they came—from different denominational backgrounds, with different personalities, and at different places in their walk with God.

A good father names his sons correctly, and I watched for signs of who they were by observing their individual gifts and talents. One was a teacher, another a musician, one an evangelist, another a missionary, still another a pastor, and another skilled in management. Of course, we didn't know this at first. When we got it wrong and tried to make the evangelist a musician or the teacher a manager, we made the necessary correction and kept moving.

My job was not that hard; I just had to remember the building process wasn't all about me. Sometimes you can be in the position of a father, but not be a father. I knew the key was to serve and create an atmosphere where these future leaders could grow. Sometimes I did it well and sometimes not so well, but we hung on to each other anyway.

We not only did church and life together, but everything in between. We camped out, went to movies, and had long discussions. Some of those discussions were great. Other times we closed with quick prayers that ended with "God bless us as we go our separate ways." We didn't agree all the time, but we always celebrated our successes with food or coffee and laughter and stories that never ended. During the week we were in the hospitals and homes of our members, teaching, encouraging, and praying. On Sunday mornings we sat together—suited up, prayed up, and ready to serve.

## Covenant Friendships

Committed covenant friendships cannot be adequately defined by a dictionary. No one uses a company rulebook to learn how to be available for a friend. When a covenant friend goes through difficult times and the chips are down, you want the friend to win, because part of your heart is invested in that person's dreams. When you're in covenant, long after the adventure, romance, or paychecks end, you and your friend will still be standing side-by-side, fighting the same enemy.

And no, of course we don't walk the aisle or make public vows such as, "I take thee, Bob, to be my everlasting friend in sickness and in health." Most of the time we don't mention the commitment. But it's there. We understand that what God has joined together for the kingdom shouldn't be torn asunder by human differences, ego competitions, or wounded trust.

One of my most beloved team members, Monty Smith, was our worship leader at Shady Grove. For multiple years, Monty led our congregation into the presence of God with a tender heart and his love for God. He lived with a compassion for the nations that launched and blessed both Shady Grove Church and other ministries around the world.

Monty had to step down from the pulpit because of personal decisions that hurt not only himself but everyone around him. My heart was broken, but our relationship remained intact. He's still my son in the gospel and remains a close friend today.

Reputations take a beating when we fail or make mistakes, but that doesn't mean our call or destiny has changed. And it shouldn't mean we let go of each other either. Why? Because God loves covenant—that's what He's known for. You'll notice Him making covenants with all sorts of people: Adam and Eve, Abraham, Moses, and the children of Israel. God works within covenant. When others break their part of the covenant, God doesn't break His.

None of us have been able to keep our promises to God to be pure and without sin. We haven't done much better than our forefathers in the obedience department. None of us obey every time or respond like Jesus in every way. Thankfully, God protects and keeps us in relationship with Himself through the covenant He made with Jesus on our behalf. It is a covenant that can't be broken, because God can't lie.

*"I will never leave you nor forsake you,"* He says in Hebrews 13:5, which shows how strong the covenant is. He holds on for both of us.

We can mirror this tenacious love to each other as long as we don't demand that others never hurt us, betray us, or talk behind our back (and the list could go on). The truth is, they probably will. We probably do. Living in covenant is costly, and it doesn't come easily to our human nature. But we can choose to forgive quickly, stand our ground with love and compassion, and wait for the Holy Spirit to bring us peace and understanding in every situation.

God assigns each of us a sphere of relationship that will further His kingdom on earth. This sphere is not always defined by geography and title, but rather by spiritual impact and growth. If we want to complete our call and assignments, and leave a lasting legacy, we have to hold on to the covenant relationships God has established in our life.

One of the greatest covenant relationships in the Bible was between two men, David and Jonathan. Jonathan's father, Saul, the king of Israel, was intent on killing David. As a result, Jonathan found himself in an awkward situation when this messy family situation and his covenant relationship with David collided. Eventually, Jonathan had to choose good over evil. He stood by his friend, protecting and defending his life.

Without knowing it, when he made a covenant with David that included laying down his life for him, Jonathan was also defending and protecting the plan of God for Israel. God had already decided David was to be king, not Saul.

David and Jonathan's roles in life changed, but not their friendship. Jonathan was royalty, and David was a soldier who bowed down to him (see 1 Samuel). Later, it was David who was king over Jonathan's offspring, and the covenant between the two men surpassed both royalty and power. Let's take a brief look at that scenario.

Though David and Jonathan knew there was a great possibility death would interrupt their friendship, they were thinking ahead to the legacy they would leave for the generations to follow: *Then Jonathan said to David, "Go in peace, since we have both sworn in the name of the Lord, saying, 'May the LORD be between you and me, and between your descendants and my descendants, forever.'" So he arose and departed, and Jonathan went into the city* (1 Samuel 20:42).

Years afterward when David became king, he was aware he would not have held the position, had Jonathan not helped save his life. In thinking about his covenant with Jonathan, who had by then died, David asked about his friend's children: *"Is there still anyone who is left of the house of Saul, that I may show him kindness for Jonathan's sake?"* (2 Samuel 9:1).

There was such a person. Jonathan's son was alive. Crippled from childhood, this "dead dog" (as the boy called himself) was living a miserable life, useless and disregarded. Though Mephibosheth had come from royalty, his present life was anything but.

When David learned of the boy's situation, he restored Mephibosheth to his position as grandson of the former king of Israel—with all the wealth, land, and servants that would have been passed down from his father, Jonathan. For the rest of his life, Mephibosheth ate at David's table as one of his sons and part of the family.

Through his father's covenant relationship with David, he was given back his name, his rightful inheritance. That's a biblical picture of covenant. It extends down through the generations and into eternity. It is legacy shared—strength multiplied and power unleashed. Covenant can withstand generational curses, fight off the enemy's hatred, evil, and vicious contempt . . . and restore destinies.

## Share the Vision

If you want to fulfill your destiny, pray for the friendships or the team you need to help get you there. Ask God for people who will see your dream and help fight your battles. Choose men and women who are faithful and loyal, and then invest in their lives. Your journey will be easier if you admit, right from the start, you don't have all the answers and you understand mistakes will be made. Keep covenant anyway.

I'm still in committed relationship with almost all of the elders from those early days at Shady Grove. I know their children, and I listen to stories about their grandchildren. I'm a part of their ministries, and we still eat together, talk, share great movies, and rehash our latest sermons.

The fruit born of these covenant friends has spread throughout the nations, from Brussels to Israel and Africa to Denmark. I cheer for these sons and grandsons as if I'm at their ball games, watching them hit their home runs. Sometimes they need me, and sometimes I need them. We're still a team.

My own life is proof positive that the walk through this life on the way to eternity is not a single, straight, perfect line. Visions sometimes need recalibrating. The winds of culture may blow a different way, demanding a fresh perspective of an established truth. The way we thought was going to be a straight sprint to the end, is not. The path we're on curves and dips through valleys, and meets up with battles we never expected.

Still, the plan of God triumphs. And when we are in covenant friendships, holding on to each other for dear life, we take territory together, and for each other.

Joe Oakley, one of my original sons in the gospel, now pastors Grace Fellowship, a thriving, worshiping church in the community of Grand Prairie, Texas. Every time I go there, I feel right at home, surrounded by familiar worship and family. Joe was an elder at Shady Grove Church who, along with his wife, Deborah, still preaches and teaches with the same passion and anointing that helped build Shady Grove.

Robert Morris, Senior Pastor of Gateway Church in Southlake, Texas, is one of my spiritual sons who was part of Shady Grove Church for sixteen years. He was on our team of elders that prayed, preached, laughed and looked out for each other. We are used to running the race together, and both of us have the same vision of seeing Christ glorified on earth. Robert is both son and friend, as well as fellow minister, and our shared vision has come full circle.

In 2013, Shady Grove Church merged with Gateway Church and became one of its several flourishing campuses. The merge seemed perfectly natural and right to all of us because we were already a family and team. (In a family, you realize that no matter what happens, family will always be family—your DNA is the same.) The vision has come full circle because what started out as an embryo of worship has now become a worldwide outreach. In addition to recording and releasing seven major worship albums, Gateway has sent worship leaders around the world to teach and train musicians and leaders.

My Scout leader, Marty Potter, had it right: if we are on a team, we serve in the position where we're needed most. In the kingdom of God, it's all about getting to the goal (glorifying God) and fighting the same enemy (Satan).

Whether we are in a covenant relationship with family, friends, or a team, the main thing is to be fluid and flexible. We never know what God is doing until we get in step with His rhythm. To keep up with Him, we will always be learning a new melody and a new beat to the same "Song of the Redeemed" that began at the cross. Our feet may stumble at first, but once we come in line with His leading, we can keep on dancing.

# CHAPTER 22

∽

# *Jerusalem First*

John Steinbeck once said Texas was so big that we Texans thought we were our own nation. He wasn't far off. I was born and raised "all things Texan," as the saying goes, and for years never concerned myself with anything but local or national issues. The rest of the globe was only interesting when a crisis flared up and made the front-page news.

The small nation of Israel was of little interest to me. Of course, I knew my history and was aware of Israel's beginnings as a nation. When I was a seminary student I studied Jesus' Jewish roots as subject and fact. But for me, the Jewish people and their nation remained just that: subject and fact. That is, until one night when I watched a television documentary on the Holocaust.

I had seen many such documentaries throughout the years, but this one was different; it changed my life. The recovered footage was of actual medical research being carried out on Jews who were still alive. Naked women and children were left in the snow in sub-zero temperatures so that "researchers" could time how long it took them to die. Jewish men were castrated without anesthesia to see how they

153

handled the pain. None of the victims looked into the camera. Instead, naked and stripped of human dignity, they kept their eyes down, their heads bowed. Their shame seemed to transverse both time and distance to come right through the screen. I wanted to apologize to them for watching, because I knew their dignity had been violated. It was a devastating experience for me.

I went outside to my prayer place, a small pump house that covered the well we used for watering the yard. I found some free floor space, laid face down, and cried out this newfound pain in my spirit. I grieved the sorrow of these people and their generations, still marked by a history of audacious torture and rejection. I prayed God would forgive my nation and every other nation that had let this happen.

For the first time, I prayed—really prayed—for the Jewish people. I stayed on my face until 3 a.m., weeping and asking God to not let the Jews be bitter, to prosper them, to take care of their little ones. I felt like I was praying for my own family.

Then I remembered God's promise to Abraham: *"I will make you a great nation; I will bless you and make your name great; and you shall be a blessing. I will bless those who bless you, and I will curse him who curses you; and in you all the families of the earth shall be blessed"* (Genesis 12:2–3).

The next day I could still hear the words buzzing in my ear: "Those who bless you (Israel), I will bless."

"I don't know how, God," I told Him, "but I will bless the Jewish people."

I was passionate about being a blessing to Israel, but what was I to do? How does a good ole boy from Texas start digging into His spiritual Jewish roots? I looked up the number for Baruch Ha Shem, a Messianic Jewish Congregation in Dallas. It was the only one I had ever heard of in our city. I called the rabbi and plunged right to the point. I told him I was a Christian pastor who wanted to serve the Jewish people, but I didn't know where to start. I asked if he could help me.

He could. It turns out he needed someone to help serve their congregation at Passover so that they could all sit down as a family for this sacred, traditional meal. A group of us went over and served our Jewish brothers and sisters with all the love and humility we felt toward Christ.

Serving a Passover meal seemed a minor thing to do, but everything that followed was a direct result of that single, seemingly small act of obedience. We heard that an Orthodox Jewish congregation had started a Thursday-night class called "The Joys of Jewish Learning." With their permission, I took some of our church members to the classes, where we learned about the customs, culture, and feasts of the Jewish nation. Without knowing it, we were taking baby steps of obedience that would change each of us forever.

Women from our church took Hebrew dance classes, and we incorporated these dances into our worship. "Strange," some people said about our worship. But our congregation loved the link with the roots and culture of our faith, so we even started tithing our offerings to Israel. We also helped launch a new Messianic Jewish congregation in New York. Still, we wanted to do more.

The more I studied the Scripture—from the prophecies of the Old Testament to the gospels in the New Testament—the more I realized that what we were doing was not a cultural-exchange program. I knew I had touched a part of the heart of God for His people: *"But go rather to the lost sheep of the house of Israel. And as you go, preach, saying 'The kingdom of heaven is at hand'"* (Matthew 10:6–7).

Wayne Wilks, a young man who came to Shady Grove Church to check out our worship, ended up becoming a member and later a part of the senior leadership team. Then a student at the University of North Texas, Wayne loved to learn and loved to teach—a combination any pastor prays to have as part of his team. When Wayne told me he was conflicted between going on to get his doctorate or staying on staff, I encouraged him to do both. I knew his degree would be used for the kingdom, so we helped support him and flexed our needs to his rigid schedule. Although it was a bit unorthodox, it was one of the best investments Shady Grove ever made.

Wayne and his wife, Bonnie, both had a passion for the Jewish people and wanted to serve in missions abroad someday. Eventually an opportunity arose for the Wilkses to pioneer a Bible school for new Jewish believers in the former Soviet Union. After the fall of communism, teams rushed in with the gospel, and thousands of Jewish people came to a true understanding of their Jewish Messiah. They needed to be trained and equipped, so the Messianic Jewish Bible Institute was formed.

We helped raise the funds for this endeavor and also for the Wilkses' personal support. In so doing, we knew we had taken our love for the Jewish people to another level. In addition, we partnered with other grounded ministries who shared our vision, and added a young Ukrainian couple with Jewish roots to our team.

A group of us, including the Wilkses and Rabbi Jonathan Bernis, head of Jewish Voice Ministries, traveled to Moscow, where we had a conference with Russian pastors. We were revved and ready to launch. But the question was, where were we going to start our first Messianic Jewish Bible institute for Jewish students? We fasted and prayed, searching for God's direction in the matter.

I woke up one morning with one name repeating in my mind: Odessa. But the only Odessa I knew was in west Texas. When our team met for breakfast that morning, I said, "Guys, I don't know what you'll think about this, but I believe we're supposed to start our first school in Odessa—though I can't imagine who would want to come to Odessa, Texas, to attend a Messianic Jewish Bible institute."

That's when I learned Odessa is a famous port on the Black Sea in the Ukraine. Exiled Russian Jews had squeezed into every boat they could find in an effort to escape the persecution sweeping through their nation.

As the team headed for Odessa, it seemed as if they were living in the book of Acts, with the Holy Spirit nudging them forward into the unknown. Sure enough, they found their place in Myaki, a small community twenty miles outside the city. They also found camp facilities on the border of Bulgaria that would be perfect for the first Jewish institute.

Odessa, Texas, was named after the original city in the Ukraine, but as far as I could tell, that's all the two cities had in common. I didn't know cold until I experienced the deep winter in the Ukraine. Everything was frozen: the river, the snow we crunched through, the pipes in the building—even our fingers and toes. Ice-cold showers in the morning made me thank Jesus that Wayne and Bonnie were the ones staying, not me. I thank God I am still called to Texas and sunshine!

Neither Wayne nor I had any idea that God's vision for him and Bonnie would grow to include so many nations. At present, he and Bonnie are still planting Messianic Jewish Bible Institutes (MBJI) in countries throughout the world, including Romania, Hungary, Argentina, Brazil, Korea, Ethiopia, and Zimbabwe.

Shady Grove Church had touched God's heart for His people, and the experience changed us, not only individually, but also as a church. Today, MJBI is an organization that still circles the globe to teach and train Messianic ministers of the gospel.

## Obedience and Trust

Legacies are established and grow through obedience. We can love others and pray all day long, but until we take the first step toward the will of God, we are not yet engaged with our destiny.

Did you notice that when God wants to launch you into something exciting, it often starts with one small, seemingly insignificant step? There are all kinds of reasons we use to excuse ourselves from obeying. Sometimes it's just not convenient. Other times, the task is too humbling or the conditions aren't right—you probably already know the drill of doubt. But when we refuse to take the first, small steps of any vision, we miss out on the adventure God intends to take us on.

> *What does it profit, my brethren, if someone says he has faith but does not have works? Can faith save him? If a brother or sister is naked and destitute of daily food, and one of you says to them, "Depart in peace, be warmed and filled," but you do not give them the things which are needed for the body, what does it profit? Thus also faith by itself, if it does not have works, is dead* (James 2:14–17).

Sometimes one single, strong prayer can be so powerful that it changes you forever. I know; it happened to me. I learned that when we catch God's heart for people, we're happy to obey His voice. Obedience and trust pay great dividends.

As for Syble and me, we go to Israel every time our schedule clears long enough for us to be gone. By faith, we've invested in a small piece of Israel's land. We go there as often as we can to teach and pray and encourage our Jewish family to hold on to their promises.

On a clear day, we can see the mountains of Moab from our apartment. Like it or not, we also have a good view of the war and unrest that goes on in Jerusalem. Sometimes we can see tires burning and police stepping in to stop fights. We hear the chanting of hateful slogans, the banging of pots and pans—a modern-day version of tribal drums.

Just to the right of our home, we can see the Mount of Olives and the original city of Jerusalem. The road to Hebron, the old pathway of the patriarchs that leads to Bethlehem, is just a few blocks away. In the early morning when the sun comes up, if I prop my head up, I can see Mount Zion.

I tell Syble that when Jesus returns, she and I could be right there, among the first to jump up and meet Him. You never know.

But one thing I do know, the promise God first made to Abraham has become a legacy for all of us today who have become Abraham's seed through our faith in Jesus Christ: *I will bless those who bless you ... and in you all the families of the earth shall be blessed* (Genesis 12:3).

# CHAPTER 23

❦

# *How Do You Say Wow in Polish?*

Even if you don't know Polish history, you can get an idea of it by the title of Poland's national anthem, "Jeszeze Polska nie Zginela" (Poland Has Not Yet Perished). If you compared the size of this small nation in central Europe to the size of a U.S. state, you'd think of Arizona. And if you compared the troubles of Poland to those of a particular person, you'd think of Job. Polish people have been invaded, killed, and dominated for generations.

Before Syble and I made our first trip to Poland in 1981, we had to look it up on the globe. It wasn't a popular European destination. No one I knew wanted to get away to Poland for fun and relaxation. Pastors and priests were being persecuted and jailed, oppression dominated the people, and hunger invaded homes and villages. Just one single fresh egg was a prized possession if they could find one.

I didn't know any of this beforehand. I only knew God wanted me to go to Poland. I had no idea how or why or when. But I knew. I told Syble that a trip to Poland was in our future, and then I waited. Dreams often begin in "our knower"—deep in our spirit—before we

161

understand all the logical details. If going to Poland was a God-given dream for my life, then He would open the doors and confirm it.

Not long afterward, when Polish businessman Robert Paripovich and his wife visited the United States, one of our church members brought them to Shady Grove. We took the couple out to dinner after the service, but Syble and I made a point not to mention our call to go to Poland. If God was speaking to us about going there, He would also confirm it in His own way.

Weeks after our new Polish friends departed, a letter written in Polish came to the church office. It took a while to get someone who could translate it. The letter was from a Polish pastor who got right to the point: he wanted me to visit his church and teach them what Robert saw when he was at your church." Evidently, Mr. Paripovich had returned to Poland and told his pastor about our worship at Shady Grove Church. Another official letter followed with an invitation from the United Evangelical Churches of Poland. This was the confirmation I was waiting for. We were going to Poland.

When our plane landed in Warsaw, tanks were on the runway and the city was on a 10 p.m. lockdown. If we had doubted it before, it was now official: we were in a communist country that was under the threat of a real revolution. Our room on the thirty-seventh floor of our hotel was small and claustrophobic. Syble looked out the window and announced, "I want to go home."

"Too late," I told her. "Whatever happens will happen. We have just made a full commitment."

Our new friend, Robert Paripovich, drove us through towns and cities with names that tangled our tongues: Bydgoszcz, Katowice, Ustron, Krakow. We were on mission and simply went from one place to the next according to the plans our hosts had made for us. As we were leaving Bydgoszcz on our way to Krakow, Robert stopped in a small village of about five hundred people. One of the members of their small church was dying of cancer, and we were asked to pray for her.

It was getting dark, and I was scheduled to preach that night in Krakow. I didn't know whether to feel honored or interrupted. I sure didn't feel like God's man of faith and power at the time, but that was beside the point. The woman needed to feel God's love, she needed a miracle, and it wasn't up to me to conjure up either one. I had come to Poland to make myself available for God to use any way He wanted to, and that's just what I did.

We walked through the thick fog to a small house. Once inside, we were led up the stairs to the woman's bedroom. The lights were dim, the walls sweating beads of condensation. A small group of Christians were playing Polish worship music and standing around a bed where the woman lay in fetal position. It was a depressing scene, dark and dank. The room even smelled of death. I felt no great faith for the moment, but I prayed anyway, and then we left.

We later learned that, the next morning, the woman had gotten up out of bed and fixed breakfast—totally healed. All I could say was *wow!* It was not my power that healed her, but God's. All I did was obey. Thank you, God.

We went on to Ustron, a town on the Czech border where two hundred people were packed into a small church pastored by a man named Hornak. Only ten minutes into my sermon, I stopped. For some reason, I felt I was to tell these people not to move from this place, that God had planted them there and He wanted them to bloom. Through a translator I said, "Pastor Hornak, you will have a building so large, you'll have a balcony section. You'll have conferences here with people coming from the nations around you. You will form a new denomination, and you will be the first president of the organization."

Even while I was saying these things, I was asking myself why. What was I doing? I had just laid out the future of the church, and I didn't even know these people. I didn't know what they believed.

Had I encouraged them, scared them, or insulted them? God knows I wasn't trying to start another organization in Poland. All I could say was, thank God, Robert was ready to drive us to the next town when this meeting was over.

We went on to Katowice, where I spoke on worship, the one thing I had come to do. The Holy Spirit's presence was so gentle and sweet that after a while, I told them, "The Holy Spirit is here, and He will instruct you now." I invited them to sing from their hearts through the Holy Spirit. The sounds were like none I'd heard before. The harmony and melodic Polish phrases blended like an orchestrated choir. I was simply a spectator, watching and listening. I wept and then laughed at the brilliance and power of the Spirit.

I soon noticed a group of people jumping up and down, and the translator pointed out a young man who had come in wearing glasses as thick as the bottom of Coke bottles. Though he was legally blind, while worshiping, he had discovered he could see perfectly without his glasses. He and his friends were so excited, they'd gone into full-blown party mode.

I was in awe of what was happening. This was the Holy Spirit's mission, and as long as I was willing to do things I'd never done before, I would get to see His miracles. Amazing. Wow!

Before the trip was over, Syble and I fell in love with the Polish people.

## A Full-circle Vision

It was never my goal to plant another Shady Grove Church in Poland. Instead, I loved the thrill of partnering with these strong Polish believers by taking teams of our church members to assist them in achieving their dreams for their own nation.

Even after twelve years of these annual mission trips, I still had a yearning to preach along the Poland-Soviet Union border. I asked my sidekick, Monty Smith, to bring his guitar and go with me. We had no itinerary. There were no great meetings planned. We would wing it, like two buddies going on an incognito adventure. Monty was an evangelist who loved to preach, and I loved to teach and lead worship. Ours relationship was an old-fashioned, book-of-Acts model, and I wanted to see how God would use us in Poland.

One morning in Warsaw, a young man came to our hotel and told us the president of a Bible college wanted to meet us. Evidently, we were not as incognito as we thought. The young man took us to a large building where we walked up the stairs and down a corridor to the president's office. To my amazement, sitting behind the desk was Pastor Hornak, whom I had met on my first trip to Poland.

He stood up and hugged me, Polish-bear-style. "Remember me?" he said with a smile. "I'm the pastor you prophesied over, twelve years ago. We wanted to move away from the Czeck border; but you told us to stay, so we did. Now I'm the president of the first Pentecostal organization to be formed in Poland, and this is our Bible school. Students and pastors come from all over eastern Europe to worship and study, just like you said."

It was a full-circle kind of moment for me. The miracle that began as a word given by faith twelve years ago had grown into a building filled with people who were impacting nations. This miracle deserved some kind of spiritual acknowledgment, but *wow* was the only thing that came to mind. So I said it: "Wow!"

Pastor Hornak was excited when we told him about our dream of evangelizing the Russian-Polish border towns. He quickly put together an itinerary of strategic, needy villages where believers were desperate for encouragement. "I'm giving you a car to use and your own driver," he told us. He even insisted on paying for our food. We were walking through our own modern-day book of Acts.

Monty and I were making this trip by faith, financially and in every other way. Within hours of arriving, our itinerary, transportation, food, and driver had all been provided. We looked at each other and said it together: "Wow!"

All along the border we preached, declared the gospel, worshiped, and prayed. We didn't know it at the time, but we were making a way for future miracles in Poland and Russia. Our part may have been small, but I knew it was strategic. Monty and I were joining with the prayers and faith and works of multiple generations of people, both before and after us, for that part of the world. Years later, when we saw the Berlin wall come down, churches and Bible schools sprang up as freedom began to grow in an oppressed nation.

Miracles like these don't just happen. God is constantly watching over the nations, moving by His Spirit, and making changes according to His plans and purposes. We may not know it at the time, but when we follow God's dreams for our individual lives, we merge with God's plan at strategic times in history to change the tide of evil. If we understood how big this plan of God's really is, we would all feel honored to have a part—any part—in it.

## The Supernatural Is Natural

While in Poland, I did things I'd never done before, things I never knew I could do. None of what happened there was of my own doing. I listened daily for God's instruction, obeyed it, and then took the next step. I learned that the supernatural occurs when heaven touches earth in the natural. The way opened up in the natural. Resources were supplied in the natural. And people's lives were changed in the natural.

I'm not an expert on the supernatural, but I know enough to recognize when it invades our world. I've learned that if I don't try to formalize the process and if I'm willing to learn how to listen through my spirit, I can experience more of the ways of God than I ever dreamed.

Here's the secret to walking in the supernatural: when the Holy

Spirit shows up, move aside and say things like, "Yes, Lord," and "How can I serve You?" He knows the past and future. He lives in eternity, discerns the human heart, and knows the circumstances surrounding everyone we meet. Because of this, He is the only one qualified to govern the nations: *But God is the Judge: He puts down one, and exalts another* (Psalm 75:7).

All God needs is someone who will work with Him—someone who will speak when He says speak, pray when He says pray, and step aside when He moves to the center of the room. For many, this is a new way of relating to the Holy Spirit; yet it's as old as the Bible. *"With men this is impossible, but with God, all things are possible,"* Jesus said in Matthew 19:26.

Living within your own logic may be safe, but ignoring the promptings of the Holy Spirit will always limit your future and cramp your dreams. Jesus told His disciples to have faith in God (see Mark 11:22). Moses didn't part the Red Sea on his own. The disciples didn't heal people; they prayed. Elijah didn't make rain; he just expected it.

Your deepest desires are a blueprint of God's dream inside you. Hold on to those desires, because when they are mixed with faith, they will propel you into the supernatural destiny you were created for.

The secret to growing our faith lies in getting to know God. John calls it *abiding*: we focus on getting to know Him and spending time in His presence. Everything else comes out of that. Everything. When we think we have to make dreams and the supernatural happen on our own, we breed our own hopelessness.

God-given ideas are always too big for us, for obvious reasons. He's God, and His plans span the generations and eternity. Miracles are His love language. There's a big difference in partnering with God and His ideas for people and nations, and in coming up with our own ideas of how our life should be. Ideas we come up with on our own have a way of moving from ideas to ideals and then to ideologies. Ideals produce pride, and ideologies produce religious rigidity.

God-given ideas are different. Somewhere, sometime, our God-given ideas have to turn into actions of faith. And when we're alone as we take the step in faith, believe me, we won't feel pride. God's dreams for us always remind us we're way too small for them. We need Him.

If your vision for your life doesn't require supernatural miracles for it to come to pass, I suggest the vision is probably too small. Think about it: You're doing God's work in the earth, partnering with a supernatural God. How could you possibly start, maintain, or finish His dreams for the earth without His supernatural intervention?

Our partnership with a supernatural God supplies all our spiritual circuits with an enlightening kind of knowing that *God works though us*. This kind of partnering experience ruins us for the mundane, predictable life we used to settle for. Now we know there's more.

I don't know how *wow* is defined in the Polish, Greek, or Hebrew languages. But I'm pretty sure it's something like, "This is so great, I don't have anything to say."

# CHAPTER 24

## *Sacred Messes*

When you believe in a supernatural God, be prepared to run into some weird people with vivid imaginations. I've met plenty, but they don't offend me. Most of them have good hearts and good intentions. Others are, well, just weird.

One minister who visited our church told me his family was especially anointed by God, and he had a picture to prove it. He handed me a photo taken when he was baptizing his son in a nearby lake under a partly cloudy sky. He said God had parted the fluffy, white clouds that day to give him a message written in ancient Greek across the sky, proving he was an apostle. He pointed to the place in the photo where I could see what indeed appeared to be some form of writing. However, the soft white letters were undecipherable.

This was obviously a supernatural sign, he told me, adding that maybe God would give me the translation. I stared at the ghostly letters, trying to remember the Greek I had studied at seminary, but the letters weren't familiar. I had never heard of anything like this is my life, but he was a minister, and I wasn't going to make fun of him.

He had extra copies of the supernatural photo, and he gave me one as a gift so that I could think about it. Syble dropped it in a junk drawer when we got home, and we both forgot about it.

Months later, as she was cleaning out the drawer, she picked up the photo and was carrying it upside down as she went to throw it away. But as she glanced at the photo she suddenly stopped—there were the words in the clouds again. But this time, from this different angle, the message was clear. The strange writing in the sky spelled out K-O-D-A-K-O-L-O-R.

We still laugh at how naive and simple our faith was in those first days of discovering the spirit realm is real. We weren't yet accustomed to operating in the supernatural dimension of our lives. The Holy Spirit was teaching us to discern what was supernatural, what was a lying wonder (see 2 Thessalonians 2:9), and what was just someone's mistaken idea of the supernatural.

In the past, although I viewed those who believed in the supernatural as extreme and didn't want to be identified with them, I was committed to knowing a supernatural God. Just because some people were extreme and scripturally ungrounded, it didn't make me question God—just them. I still wanted more of God and His Spirit within me. So I kept pursuing Him in prayer and by taking time to meditate on His Word and His attributes.

I wanted to impact my world, and I knew it meant mentoring and discipling Christ-followers who would neither stay in the shallow water of religion nor go out to a whacky-deep faith that had no scriptural foundation.

I've learned that to help people build their dreams and fulfill their destinies, you have to start with where you are—and where they are—and go from there. To have vision is to see something not yet visible, something not yet fully formed—not in you and not in them. But when the vision is based on a word from God, you know it *will* one day be fulfilled, so you move toward it: *"So shall My word be that goes forth from My mouth; it shall not return to Me voice, but it shall accomplish what I please, and it shall prosper in the thing for which I sent it"* (Isaiah 55:11).

One of the first couples I mentored at Shady Grove Church was young, fun, and newly married. Phil and Connie were also new in the faith but passionate about God. Every time the church doors were open (and sometimes when they weren't), they were there. During the rebuilding phase that followed the fire, they put on their jeans and pounded nails, brought food, and fasted and prayed—whatever was needed. All of it was always needed.

Phil and Connie rode a Harley. One day they were on their bike at a gas station when a young man pulled up in his car. Harleys are always conversation pieces, and the three started talking. Phil was looking for an opportunity to share his faith, so he plunged right in, telling the guy about how Jesus had changed his life. As the conversation progressed, both Phil and Connie realized the man needed counseling, so they led him over to our nearby church building to talk.

Our unfinished building had no electricity at the time, and it was filled with sawhorses, ladders, and freshly cut planks of wood scattered about. The poor guy didn't know where he was or even who these people were, so he did the right thing. He asked. Connie proudly announced, "This is our new church!" and pulled up a nail keg for him to sit on.

Surrounded by nails and sawdust, the young man was desperate as he sat there and poured out his life to a couple of strangers in that dark, half-built church. Phil and Connie knew he was sad, but they had no idea the seriousness of his emotional condition. "I would have already taken my life by now," he told them. "But I don't know what to do with my cat."

Connie was so stunned by the seriousness of the situation at hand that she said nothing. But in his God-given desire to help others, Phil thoughtlessly declared, "We'll take the cat!"

The counseling session had just gone south. Although it wasn't his intention, Phil had just removed the guy's last obstacle to suicide. Both Phil and Connie knew they were in over their heads. Phil called immediately for one of our church elders, and the couple kept the young man glued to the nail keg until help arrived. The elder who came to the church that day listened to the young man's story, and then gently and confidently led him to the Lord. Over the coming weeks, the elder ministered to both the man and his family, walking them successfully through their situation.

We've laughed with Phil and Connie over their first ministry session many times, but the incident proved to be an embryonic picture of who God had called them to be. Their faith continued to grow and they became our youth pastors at Shady Grove Church. Years later, one of their seven children, Josh, became our youth pastor before going on to be a part of our senior leadership team. Josh is in leadership now at Gateway Church. The legacy God established in Shady Grove Church was passed not only to Phil and Connie but also to the generations that followed them.

As our own vision and call unfolds before us, it continues to transfer to others, calling them to their destiny as well. Sometimes the transfer is almost imperceptible. Nevertheless, our love and passion for God, lived day in and day out, is the most powerful seed we have, and so we remain committed to the process—both in ourselves and in the people we are mentoring. There is a time of interceding and waiting, of loving and holding on—no matter what. Being part of someone else's growth process is not always exciting or even pleasant. Thus we endeavor to keep before our eyes the apostle Paul's description of the experience: *my little children, for whom I labor in birth again until Christ is formed in you* (Galatians 4:19).

## Giving Birth in the Spirit

The birth of a call is a sacred movement of life and always needs tender-loving care. Nothing of worth can be successfully birthed if we are taking an exam on performance at the same time. The birth experience is natural, a little messy, and always wonderful if we have eyes to see what the Holy Spirit is doing.

Nurturing each other's calls means we are there for support and back-up—not to direct or own another person's experience. We're not trying to fill the world with countless variations of "miniature me's." There's room for all the personality colors of the rainbow and all the miraculous gifts of God's grace. The glory of God—the light of God—shines through every one of us in a myriad of different ways.

I'm of the old-school thinking that says when we limit our partners in ministry only to those who have degrees and experience, we risk giving birth to a facsimile of what God intends for us or, worse yet, a stillbirth.

Jesus could see the potential for leadership that would change the world in two tough, redneck fishermen. *"Follow Me, and I will make you fishers of men"* (Matthew 4:19), He said to Simon Peter and his brother, Andrew, as soon as He met them. How could they possibly have known they would one day be teaching, preaching, casting out devils, and performing miracles? How could anyone have seen an author of the New Testament in one of them? Nobody could possibly have known those two fishy-smelling, not-educated-at-school guys would still be impacting our lives today.

Amazing miracles, yet to come forth, are hidden inside the people of our household and those at our school, our job, and our church. These people might not know it yet, but they are waiting for us to catch the vision. Not our vision, but God's vision. If we are confident of who we are, we can call forth from them the same Spirit of God that resides in us. No one, not even God, expects us to shape their vision.

All we have to do is recognize it and call it forth; God will do the rest.

When I was eleven years old, I was asked to close a Boy Scout meeting in prayer. I had never prayed out loud in front of anyone—ever. My heart was pounding like a machine gun and my face was red, but I prayed anyway.

Afterward, I was so embarrassed, I wanted to hide. My prayer was too choppy, not smooth like they did it in church. I wasn't sure how to end it, so I ran my words together at the end: "In-the-name-of-Jesus-amen." I didn't want to look at anyone, so I stared at the floor and headed toward the door.

But then I felt an arm slip around my shoulder and heard the voice of the pastor who sponsored our Boy Scout troop: "Olen, I believe that was one of the best prayers I have ever heard," he said. At the same time, my Scout leader walked up and affirmed that, yes, it was true: I had just prayed one of the best prayers of all time. Who knew? I was a pray-er. I could probably be a leader too. I went home walking on air because those two men had just called forth a new vision in my mind of who I was. And sure enough, here I am today, a pray-er and a leader.

Vision plus discernment plus words equals a powerful combination. God used this combination in Genesis to create the world out of chaos. Because we are made in the image of God, we have the ability to establish His kingdom on earth with the same combination of vision, discernment, and words. When we live out our vision in this life, we are establishing a legacy that calls into being the dreams of others, which, in turn, shapes the kingdom of God on earth.

# CHAPTER 25

&

# *Generational Anointing*

It was all right as far as Christmases go. Not great, but okay. Our son, Mark, his daughter, Heather, and our two grandsons, who lived nearby, had plans elsewhere for the day. All of our other children, grandkids, and greats were in Belgium, where they lived at the time. Syble and I would have to have a Merry Christmas anyway—on our own.

We drove to San Antonio and checked into a hotel near the lights and festivities of downtown and the River Walk. We knew not to expect anything like snow or mistletoe or children's toys under the tree. But we were looking forward to lit-up trees, some beautiful Christmas carols, and great Mexican food.

Before the day was over, both of us were teary-eyed and bewailing our miserable holiday. We talked about having our children and grandchildren and greats around the tree. We remembered Syble's Christmas cinnamon rolls baking in the oven and the chaos of having a house filled with family. Why, oh why, were we not with them? What new low had we dropped to that brought us to a place where we were walking with tourists from Minnesota, singing "I Saw Mommy Kissing Santa Claus"?

175

We promised ourselves this would never happen again, and it was a promise we kept. The next year we dropped everything and hopped on a plane to Brussels. We had learned our lesson: there are no substitutes for family.

Our family connections are established through bloodline, history, and tradition that we hand down from generation to generation. We are a collective lump of clay in a unique mold, stamped with the family DNA—a passport into the inner circle. No matter how far we've flown from the nest or how long we've been gone, we will always belong to each other. My great-great-grandchildren will be linked to my legacy forever. They will have something about them—the shape of their head, the color of their hair, or a mannerism they never observed or learned from me—that's in their genes naturally.

I've watched Jerri and Gary, my daughter and son-in-law, as they held their own grandbabies for the first time, looking for signs of the family stamp on the next generation. "Look," they coo, "she has her mother's eyes," or "Boy, you can tell he's a Benjamin." I've learned to step back at these times and let the grandparents take the stage, full and center. Rightly so. For Syble and me, the joy of great-grandbabies is a generational one. We get to watch our own grown children make silly faces and strange sounds just like we did. It's gooey grandparent love pouring down on the next generation of grandparents.

Brand-new grandbabies and great-grandbabies make you realize that a part of you is being passed down, rebirthed. Prior decisions, which didn't seem like a big deal at the time, will frame part of this new life. Your stories will be retold, your faith relived. But this time it will be through them, with their unique individual twist. That's how legacy works.

Jerri and Gary took the legacy we handed down to them, created their version of it, and then handed it down again. They established the House of Prayer ministry at Shady Grove Church, a ministry that prayed for the needs of the church and its members, and taught others how to pray powerful and effective prayers. Jerri and Gary pray over their five children, laugh and twitter like crazy, and do ministry together. When they're not around, Syble and I take credit for how beautiful and godly their children are, how fun and witty and talented we made them. Of course, we fool no one. They bear their parents' image.

Yet I see my own father's faith in them. The part of Dad that wanted so passionately to minister the gospel is now in his great-grandsons. Dad enrolled in seminary when I was a teenager, and he planted small churches in west Texas. Although he didn't live to see it, his great-grandsons have the same passion. They've planted themselves in different soil, but they have the same faith. They have a broader view of the world, a fuller understanding of the diversity of gifts and calls and anointing than their great grandfather had. But the seed came down through him and their other great grandfather, Aaron Rose.

I took my father's strong, well-rooted Baptist faith and carved out my own life plan. My father's faith was the best gift he gave me—not perfect, but exactly what I needed to grow my own faith. My yearning to know a supernatural God through extravagant worship was what I handed down to my grandchildren, and theirs after them. Every step of faith Syble and I took was recorded and expanded on.

Gary Benjamin, my son-in-law, is a godly man who, along with my daughter, has raised all of his children to believe that everything is possible with God. Though they currently live in the Dallas-Fort Worth area, there was a time when they uprooted their comfortable, safe lives and planted their dream seeds in Europe's soil. They lived by faith—thousands of miles away from some of their children and grandchildren—and were bold enough to believe that radical faith would change the world. Their call to bring revival to Europe's youth was radical, and my dad would be blown away if he could see their lives and ministry.

Not long ago Syble and I visited a large church that has numerous campuses across the country, as well as being on the Internet. We found our seats and then waited for the moment our grandson Austin would take the stage and lead his team of musicians and the large congregation into worship. I wept as we began to worship, though I didn't know if it was because of the presence of the Lord or the fact that my grandson had caught the passion for worship. Our grandson Landon—in another megachurch—is a worship leader too, with a spirit so soft and tender toward the God he loves and serves. And our third grandson, Preston, is on staff with a discipleship training school in Herrnhut, Germany. Our granddaughter Destiny and her family were missionaries in Belgium. Another granddaughter Courtney and her husband minister here in the states with AOI (Antioch Oasis International), a network of pastors and leaders that I have led for twenty-eight years.

None of these grandchildren were in Seattle with me when I first realized worship would always be the foremost passion of my life. Their parents didn't coerce, cajole, or insist they go into ministry. But when you and I live out our vision and call, we always open the door for others around and after us to live out theirs. Our individual call has a supernatural life and anointing that sustains us through the bumps, failures, and discouragements of this life. Legacy, at its best, is handed down and around while we're still alive. Then, if we're blessed beyond anything we could have ever imagined—like I am—we get to watch when it multiplies. There's nothing like it.

# CHAPTER 26

∽∾

# *The Speech of Angels*

Church has come a long way since I was a young boy. I grew up thinking it was the capital of a place called Boring. Sundays were the day I had to get up early, dress up, and then sit down for most of the morning (from 9:45 a.m. until noon). If the closing prayer didn't come at noon on the dot, we got nervous. The Methodists in town would beat us all to the local restaurants.

I listened to the same people say the same thing (from what I could tell) over and over. The same offering plate was passed, the same announcements were read about Wednesday night service and the monthly potluck and who would like to bless the congregation and mow the grass.

I don't know why, but we kept a board up on the wall of our church beside the choir loft, telling us how many people came for Sunday school and how much was given in the offering. I thought the board was a little depressing, especially when the numbers were down, but at least everything was out in the open. Except, of course, the things that weren't.

The one part of the service that could have been fun was the music. I always thought listening to music, any kind of music, was better than listening to somebody talk. But Sister Hazel sat at the same bench at the same upright piano and played the same notes from the same red Baptist hymnal. Every week. There were no variations, no key changes, no creative cords. It was as if the notes had showed up to do the minimal amount of work and nothing else.

I had no idea why we sang about bringing in the sheets until I learned the real words were "bringing in the sheaves." Still, what were sheaves? And why were singing about them?

## Personal and Corporate

Years later—make that decades later—as I sat in Shady Grove Church (the church I pastored) with my eyes closed and the sounds of the small orchestra washing over me, I couldn't help but smile as I remembered myself as a boy, thinking church was boring and singing "bringing in the sheets." Now worship was the highlight of the week for me as hundreds of people filled the sanctuary and, together, we sang out our "heart love" to God.

Although we worshiped God corporately, the experience was deeply personal. Almost everyone responded to the Holy Spirit with his or her own personal style. Some worshiped with a quiet dignity. Others wept their way through a whole song. Some swayed to the music, their hands lifted in worship.

The worship leader at the podium led the congregation much like a conductor leads a great choir, only the emphasis was not on the performance or even the musical score. No one had practiced beforehand, yet the sounds of that worship filled the atmosphere with harmony and an electric expectancy. We were waiting on God, taking time to thank Him, love Him, and adore Him.

Sometimes this kind of worship made us want to get up and

dance like no one was watching us, so we did. Other times the same blended notes made us want to bow low at the majesty and wonder of God. So we did.

Coming together with all of us offering our individual sound to the Holy Spirit's melody turned the tired mundaneness of our lives into a supernatural experience. Church members and visitors visibly relaxed. One could almost see burdens drop and bow in that atmosphere where God ruled.

Call us crazy, but during times like I just described, the whole congregation felt the Spirit of God as if we could reach out our hands and touch Him. This should not be a foreign thought, especially since the psalmist declared that God is enthroned in the praises of His people (see Psalm 22:3).

## One Accord, One Place

How does this kind of worship happen? How do you shut out the world and see God reigning over His universe? The answer is tucked into a short verse in the New Testament: *When the Day of Pentecost had fully come, they were all gathered in one accord in one place* (Acts 2:1).

Worship is just that simple: one place, one accord. One definition of *accord* is "harmony of sounds; agreement in pitch and tone; agreement of opinion and will and action."

During times of worship, we are not giving our different opinions or criticizing a sermon or person. Worship won't let us feel inferior to others (it's not about us). And when we worship, we don't compare ourselves to others (it's not about them).

Unity is the supernatural miracle that happens when the Holy Spirit directs our gaze toward Jesus and the Father. For those moments (or hours) when we are pouring out our love to Jesus and the Father, we are not thinking of how to be first or how to get ahead. God takes up all the space in our minds.

## One Pure Note

Our part in worship is this: we find our spirit-voice and sing out our one pure note from the purest, innermost place inside us. That's all God wants from us. He does the rest.

The Spirit takes each individual note and creates a masterpiece for God. Every note is needed. A note coming out of the mouth of a child is different from the note of a teenager who "rocks it." A rich bass note booming forth from a six-foot-tall man is not the same as the quivering soprano note of an aged grandmother. The Holy Spirit takes our individuality and merges us into a corporate experience that fills the heavens and the earth with the sound of God. We are joining the myriads of angels around the throne of God.

Anything can happen in this atmosphere. Healing. Salvation. Restoration of relationships. Faith reborn. Vision. Revelation. Understanding. God's natural habitat is worship. When we are in one place and in one accord, He shows up.

One Greek word for liturgy, or worship, is *leitourgia*. This term actually derives from two words that mean "all the people" and "action." All the people—not a few priests or one preacher at the podium— participate in one action, one common goal: worship. This is liturgy at its best. When we come together and add our individual note to the corporate worship of God, we build a bridge (action) together (all the people). This bridge of worship always connects the natural with the supernatural.

Our one pure note, mixed in melodious harmony with others, creates a wave of praise that makes God laugh joyously at the sound reaching His throne room. Finally—through praise and worship—we have created a true space for Him.

When I look back at the young boy who yawned through those church songs of childhood, I now realize there was nothing wrong with Sister Mildred or her upright piano. The notes were correct. But no matter how well she played them, there was only one person playing. The rest of us were mainly spectators doing the same thing over and over. Week after week the sound remained unchanged. No one messed with the formula, which was this: don't mess with the formula.

Worship was never intended to be dead or boring. We tend to make it that way ourselves, all by ourselves. And now that I know I have the ability to enter into true worship, I don't do boring anymore. I go throughout my day and into every church service with my spirit standing on tiptoe, asking, what is God saying now, present tense?

If life is tough—and it is—then I need to be assured again and again that He is greater than my problems. Worship does this for you and me. Once you experience God's presence, you will never be satisfied until you experience Him some more. The presence of God ruins you for anything that doesn't measure up to the experience.

And nothing ever does.

# CHAPTER 27

## Running Your Race of Faith

In the "50 Stunning Olympic Moments of All Time," Eric Liddell comes in as number 8. He won two Olympic gold medals and inspired the story for the Oscar-winning movie *Chariots of Fire*. Not many people remember the Olympics of 1924, but Liddell's name has held its own as one of the all-time greats in running.

Liddell was from the small country of Scotland, a true amateur. No one had heard of him before, the Scotsman with the awkward, sprawling stride. When he ran, Liddell threw his head back, kept his mouth open, and clawed at the air as if he were fighting with space. There was no glistening elegance to watch, no grace in his gait. Instead, people laughed and labeled him the ugliest runner to win an Olympic championship.

In one of his Olympic races, Liddell was placed on an outside track where he couldn't see the other runners well. On top of that, the games were in Paris that year and, unfortunately for the athletes, the city was in a full-blown, crippling heat wave. In one race alone, three ambulances were called to carry off the athletes (twelve of them)

185

whose unconscious bodies littered the track. You can only imagine what this did to Liddell's confidence.

But he ran his race anyway. Liddell threw his head back, jutted his chin, and flashed past the finishing tape, beating the record for the 400-meters final at 47.6 seconds. When the reporters asked him how he overcame the odds, Liddell said, "I run the first 200 meters as hard as I can. Then, for the second 200 meters, with God's help, I run harder."

I love this story because it's a great description of the race of life run by all believers. No matter how hard we practice for it, no one can predict the obstacles that will come against us. And Liddell had it right: we can't slack off when it gets tough. With God's help, we have to run harder.

## Own Your Race

We seldom look good when we're giving all we've got to our race of life. Sweat pours. The body aches. We may stumble over something we didn't see. Sometimes we fall because our legs buckle while we're running. We have to get right back up, embarrassed and humiliated. Other times people whiz by us on the way to their dreams, like they're on some kind of heavenly escalator. Their lane looks like the fast track to Jesus, and we wonder how we missed it.

And sometimes, like Liddell, we pass the bodies of those who didn't make it to the finish line. Something hindered them—physically, spiritually, or emotionally—and they gave up.

Everybody's race is a different experience; you can't compare yourself with those whizzing past you or those who lag behind. Your race is about *you*. Spectators may cheer or jeer, but your race is not about them either.

When Eric Liddell decided he wanted to be a missionary to what was then a remote part of China instead being a star athlete, Scotland

and the world were shocked. Why would he throw away a stunning sports career? Perhaps it was his legacy, passed down by his father, James Liddell, who was a missionary to China. Evidently, Eric took the baton that came from his spiritual lineage instead of the one offered him on the track.

Once, when asked to give a speech on his success as a runner, Liddell simply led the crowd in a song: "Jesus Shall Reign Where'er the Sun." He ended up in Xiaochang, China, which became a treacherous battleground with the Japanese invasion. Eric Liddell, the great Olympic runner, was captured and spent his last days as a prisoner of war in a Japanese internment camp. He was separated from his wife and children. Sick, thin, and dressed in rags, his last words to the nurse who was at his side were, "It's complete surrender."

Sometimes we have to ask ourselves, "Do I want to look like I'm succeeding, or do I want to go for the real prize that lies beneath the shiny one?" There's always a cost when we chose the eternal, weighty one: *For our light affliction, which is but for a moment, is working for us a far more exceeding and eternal weight of glory* (2 Corinthians 4:17).

Until we understand the weight of glory, we may become overwhelmed with the length of the race, the obstacles that pop up all along the way, and the ever-present fatigue that screams for us to give up.

When we are financially strapped, it's not unusual for us to think there's no way out, or to become bored with the marriage and want to get out, or tired of the burdens and want to throw them off. Being obedient to the heavenly vision God has given us when others slack off is not a little jaunt in the park. Worshiping God when He doesn't seem near is not for the faint of heart. Choosing the right race and never giving up—now that's for the strong of heart.

## Work Your Vision

Whatever it is God has put into your heart to accomplish, don't give up until it's done. Work your vision. Don't let go of the dream; it's a part of God in you. A great vision requires tough-as-nails tenacity so that you don't let it out of your sight until it's accomplished.

When Elijah, the great Old Testament prophet, was leaving this world, his protégé, Elisha, stayed nearby. In fact, he wouldn't even let Elijah out of his sight, and for good reason: they were buddies, friends, and fellow prophets. Prophets seldom have many friends, and Elisha hated to lose his spiritual mentor and guide.

But there was another reason Elisha wouldn't let his friend out of his sight: Elijah's legacy was Elisha's future. He wanted the miracles and the supernatural working in his life, just like they had in Elijah's. No Sunday-school-mild meetings for Elisha. He wanted to be able to float an ax head if he needed to (see 2 Kings 6), raise somebody up from the grave (see 1 Kings 17), or bring down water from heaven (see James 5:18). He wanted what he saw in Elijah's life.

His reasoning was brilliant: if Elijah was going to be with God, then why not leave all that power on earth? Yet his request was outrageous and passed all the boundaries of polite end-of-life transactions: "I want what you have, plus double," he told Elijah with an almost presumptuous boldness (see 2 Kings 2:9). Elijah's mantle, just as it was, would make a powerful legacy. But this was not the time to mince words; both men knew the whirlwind that would take Elijah to heaven was coming.

If Elijah had expected Elisha's request, he didn't let on. "You ask for a hard thing," he told Elisha. "Still, if you see me when I go, you can have it. If not, then no, you don't get it" (see 2 Kings 2:10). That was pretty straightforward talk between two friends. The level of their intimacy was apparent in Elijah's reply: the double-potent legacy came with stipulations.

Elijah was Elisha's vision of himself in the future, and he wasn't about to let his future out of his sight—not even when Elijah commanded him to not follow. When the whirlwind took Elijah, Elisha wouldn't be looking at the wild blue yonder.

Today's movie producers would have loved the moment: there they were, the two prophets, having their last conversation when suddenly, Elijah was literally swooped up and swirled into the heavens. Afterwards, Elisha picked up his prophet-friend's coat and his anointed legacy at the same time.

But did he really have it? Was the power really passed down? There was only one way to find out. Elisha walked to the Jordon River, struck the water with Elijah's coat, and cried out a passionate challenge: "Where is the God of Elijah?"

God said something like, "I'm right here," and then the waters parted, just as they had for Elijah. (See complete story in 2 Kings 2.)

Elisha got his supernatural legacy from his "prophet friend" who believed in a supernatural God. But it required a tenacious obedience and determined focus—all the way to the end.

If you want to live out and leave a powerful legacy that impacts generations after you, you can't get distracted by the length of the race or the hardships that come upon you unexpectedly. Stay focused. Be bold enough to ask big favors. Believe God has complete control of all the powers of the universe that He created. Believe He is on your side.

Your personal heartaches and present challenges are not indicators of your spiritual relationship with God. He's not sitting in the heavens, angry with mankind. *"In the world you will have tribulation,"* Jesus told us candidly. But in the same breath, He also said, *"But be of good cheer, I have overcome the world"* (John 16:33).

One of my personal heroes is Polycarp, a man whose life is well documented. He was one of the early church leaders who lived at the end of the age of the original apostles. Mentored by the apostle John, Polycarp was a leader of the Church in Smyrna, a town in modern

Turkey. While Christians were making the critical transition to the second generation of believers, Polycarp, a seasoned veteran of the faith, was right there, testifying of Christ and keeping order in the churches.

When he was eighty-six years old, Roman soldiers arrested him for his faith, demanding he renounce Christ as a myth and declare Caesar to be God. Polycarp's answer still speaks loudly to believers today: "Eighty-six years I have served Christ, and He never did me any wrong. How can I blaspheme my King who saved me?"[1] They burned Polycarp at the stake, but while they were stacking the wood, he offered this prayer:

"O Lord God Almighty, Father of your blessed and beloved Son Jesus Christ, through whom we have been given knowledge of yourself; you are the God of angels and powers, of whole creation, and of all generations of the righteous who live in your sight. I bless you for granting me this day and hour, that I may be numbered among the martyrs, to share in the cup of your Anointed and to rise again to everlasting life, both in body and in soul, in the immortality of the Holy Spirit. May I be received among them this day in your presence, a sacrifice rich and acceptable, even as you appoint and foreshadow, and now bring to pass, for you are the God of truth in whom there is no falsehood. For this, and for all else, I praise you, I bless you, I glorify you; through our eternal High Priest in heaven, your beloved Son Jesus Christ, by whom and through whom be glory to you and the Holy Spirit, now and for all ages to come. Amen." [2]

1   www.polycarp.net
2   pastorchrisowens.wordpress.com

That one prayer, which has been translated into multiple languages, has reverberated around the world, and it still carries a worshipful anointing that has survived the centuries. No one speaks of a Caesar religion today, but Polycarp's life and Christian faith still send a clear and loud message that never gets snuffed out. Polycarp reminds us that our Christian faith is not always popular with others, but it is founded and grounded on a truth that's worth dying for.

## Your Legacy, Your Song

No two legacies look exactly the same. Polycarp's legacy was different from mine, and mine is different from yours. You don't have to be a martyr or pastor to leave the kind of legacy that will impact generations for years to come. You just need to be a man or woman whose heart is knitted to the heart of God through His Son, Jesus Christ. Really, it's just a matter of how we respond to unexpected situations. If you are willing to be obedient to God's leading in your life, the Holy Spirit will do the rest.

But I have to warn you, get ready for a roller-coaster ride as God unfolds before you a life you could never have imagined outside of Jesus. Yes, there will be battles—but the victories that follow will be exhilarating. You will experience many different seasons in your life. The Bible says there is a time to weep and a time to laugh; a time to mourn and a time to dance; a time of war and a time of peace; a time to lose and a time to gain (see Ecclesiastes 3). Yet it is in these very battles and seasons that our own legacy song is forged.

We may be ordinary people, but we serve an extraordinary God whose plan is to use our lives to make a supernatural impact on future generations.

# ABOUT THE AUTHOR

Olen Griffing was saved in 1970 at the age of thirty-one. The son of a Baptist pastor, Olen answered the call from God to pastoral ministry shortly thereafter. He graduated from Southwestern Baptist Theological Seminary in 1972, and later became the founding pastor of Shady Grove Baptist Church in Grand Prairie, Texas.

After serving as an apostolic elder at Gateway Church in Southlake, Texas, Olen joined the team as a pastor on staff in 2012. He now prays and serves alongside the leadership of Gateway Church in the role he fills as the "spirit of a father."

Olen Griffing believes that walking in integrity, transparency, and simplicity before God allows believers to respond to life's unexpected situations in a way that transfers the love and faithfulness of God into the lives of others.

His personal values are reflected in his commitment to team ministry, his seeking the manifest presence of God, and his pursuit of foundational truths as a pathway to fulfilling the Great Commission. His heart for people was birthed from one of his favorite life scriptures: *Ask of Me and I will give You the nations for Your inheritance, and the ends of the earth for Your possession* (Psalm 2:8).

In addition to his service at Gateway Church, Olen Griffing is also the founding apostolic leader of Antioch Oasis International Network (www.aoinetwork.com), a national network committed to strengthening and establishing churches and ministries both domestically and globally.

Olen and his wife, Syble, have two children, six grandchildren, and eleven great-grandchildren. They both enjoy family activities, and they love watching as the legacy they have been called to build unfolds in their succeeding generations.

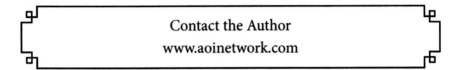

Contact the Author
www.aoinetwork.com

CPSIA information can be obtained
at www.ICGtesting.com
Printed in the USA
FFOW05n0949011114